Rural Delivery

Real Photo Postcards from Central Pennsylvania

1905-1935

Major financial sponsorships in support
of this project were received from:

Bucknell Association for the Arts
Buffalo Valley Telephone Company
McDonalds of Lewisburg and Mifflinburg
Mifflinburg Bank and Trust Company
Mifflinburg Bicentennial Committee
New Berlin Heritage Association
Q-E Manufacturing Company
West Milton State Bank

Shriner's Island, Buffalo Creek,
Lewisburg, Pa. Aug. 4, 1906.

Union Seminary

At
Allenwood
Pa.

Rural Delivery

Real Photo Postcards from Central Pennsylvania 1905-1935

Jody Blake and Jeannette Lasansky

Union County Historical Society

ACKNOWLEDGMENTS

In 1975 photo enthusiast Eric G. Stewart retired from a career in the U.S. Department of State and returned to Lewisburg, Union County, where he grew up as the son of Bucknell University biology professor Norman Stewart. Eric was eager to offer his photographic skills to local groups, and he became intent on photographing private collections of old photographs and postcards. When he moved to Oregon in 1981, Eric donated his large slide and photograph collections to the Union County Historical Society. This book is dedicated to Eric G. Stewart, whose enthusiasm and appreciation of the medium of photography have inspired others to follow in his footsteps.

More recently, those who shared real photo postcards with us include Richard D. and Leah Bingaman, the Bucknell University Archives, Carl R. Catherman, Harold T. Catherman, J. Randall Chambers, Thomas R. Deans, Janice C. Dreese, Ronald P. and Beatrice S. Dreese, Joseph Epler, Betty Hagey Herald, Sharon Herald, Helen Hopp, Donald F. Kline, Barry Knauer, Helen Kurtz, Patricia Longley, Billy and Lindy Mattern, Jeffrey L. Mensch, Ronald Nornhold, Joseph Prah, Kenneth A. and Dorothy G. Reish, Katherine Roush, Joan Sample, Delphia Shirk, Tony Shively, Gary W. and Donna M. Slear, Ethyl V. Sikes, Norman and Peggy Gundy Ulmer, John Van Buskirk, and Ruth Anna Billmeyer Zimmermann. Without their participation this project would not have been possible.

Others whose knowledge of Union County proved helpful were Judy Blair, Robert and Lucy Donehower, Paul Ernst, Mary Belle Lontz, Jack McLaren, Katherine Roush, Ethel D. Ruhl, and Ruth Wehr Zimmerman. Sharon Herald was especially helpful in securing cards from Hagey and Heiser family collections.

Assisting Jody Blake, Assistant Professor of Art History at Bucknell University, were her students and Knight Fellows: Sarah Andrews, Tom Granite, Josh Klatt, and Lara Spingler; as well as Will Heron. Also providing material were Lynn Cazabon, Assistant Professor of Art, Bucknell University; Ann Gibson at Inter-Library Loan, Ellen Clarke Bertrand Library, Bucknell University; Debbie Keefer, Alumni Records and Inventory Assistant, Bucknell University; Janice Madhu, Photo Collection, George Eastman House, Rochester, New York; Nancy Sherbert, Curator of Photographs, Kansas History Center, Topeka, Kansas; and Jean Simmons, Associate Librarian, International Museum of Photography and Film, George Eastman House, Rochester, New York.

Especially helpful were Doris Dysinger, Curator of Special Collections, Ellen Clarke Bertrand Library at Bucknell University; as well as Melissa Aukerman and Gary W. Slear of the Union County Historical Society.

Chandler Blackington, Diana Lasansky, William Lasansky, Patricia Longley, and Elsbeth Steffensen were readers for the project. Jean M. Ruhl was the copy editor.

Major financial sponsorships were received from the Bucknell Association for the Arts, the Buffalo Valley Telephone Company, McDonalds of Lewisburg and Mifflinburg, the Mifflinburg Bank and Trust Company, the Mifflinburg Bicentennial Committee, the New Berlin Heritage Association, Q-E Manufacturing Company, and the West Milton State Bank. These organizations and businesses have made a major commitment to the preservation, interpretation, and presentation of history. We thank them for their interest and support of this particular project. In addition, the Citizens' Electric Company sponsored the book's promotional flyer.

Last but not least, the bequest of the Union County Historical Society's late president, Joseph Gutelius Foster, provided the financial confidence to proceed with this very special endeavor. His belief in and commitment to local history will always be greatly appreciated.

Jody Blake and Jeannette Lasansky

Editor: Jean M. Ruhl
Layout: Jeannette Lasansky
Printer: Donning Company Publishers, Virginia Beach, Virginia

Library of Congress Cataloging-in-Publication Data
Blake, Jody, 1953-
    Rural Delivery : real photo postcards from central
Pennsylvania, 1905-1935 / Jody Blake and Jeannette Lasansky.
    p. cm.
    Includes bibliographical references (p.   ) and index.
    ISBN 0-917127-09-9
    1. Union County (Pa.) — Pictorial works.   2. Postcards —
Pennsylvania — Union County.   I. Lasansky, Jeannette.
II. Union County Historical Society (Pa.) III. Title.
F157.U5B53   1996   96-4372
974-8'48041'0222 — dc20   CIP

FRONT COVER John Reamer and his pet goose were regularly seen together in the 1910s when they were carting the mail between the post office on Market Street and the two train depots in Lewisburg. The mail was dispatched fifteen times and received fourteen times a day, Monday through Saturday. From the collection of the Union County Historical Society # 82.2.86.

BACK COVER *The Complete Directory and Post Office Guide: Lewisburg, West Lewisburg, and Four Rural Routes* was issued by the Lewisburg postmaster, W. E. Housel, in May 1911. The 100-page booklet lists all post office box holders, city residents, as well as those who lived on the rural routes. Pages 87-88 of the *Directory* delineate the exact routes of the carriers. The Rural Free Delivery carriers reported for duty each morning at 7:15 and left on their routes at 7:45. "Topography of Rural Routes" is reproduced in part here. From the collection of William and Jeannette Lasansky.

INSIDE COVER The backs of postcards are often as interesting as their fronts. From the collection of Gary W. and Donna M. Slear.

Contents

LEFT TITLE PAGE Clockwise: A cyanotype of Shriner's Island (near Campbell's Mill, formerly Steese's) on Buffalo Creek near Lewisburg. The photograph was possibly taken by Nelson F. Davis on August 4, 1906. From the collection of Gary W. and Donna M. Slear.•

The Oaklyn School House was photographed c. 1907. The school, which closed in the 1930s, has since been converted into a private home and stands at the rear service gate to the Northeastern Federal Penitentiary outside of Lewisburg on Colonel John Kelly Road. From the collection of Gary W. and Donna M. Slear.•

"Leisure time in Allenwood" was produced as early as 1907. From the collection of Thomas R. Deans.•

Union Seminarians Jay Napp and friend were photographed, c. 1908-1909, in a dormitory room in New Berlin. From the collection of Billy and Lindy Mattern.•

RIGHT TITLE PAGE Clockwise: Five young men posed on a pile of railroad ties east of Mifflinburg in 1907 or later. From the collection of Billy and Lindy Mattern.•

A winter view of the completed free bridge in Lewisburg was taken c. 1907. The water towers or "stand pipes," as well as the steeple of the First Presbyterian Church on Market Street form a familiar silhouette. The site of the former Montandon/Lewisburg cross-cut canal is still visible in the foreground. From the collection of Kenneth A. and Dorothy G. Reish.•

A hand-tinted real photo postcard of New Berlin's Main Street features the parsonage of the Lutheran Church. The post mark is 1907. The correspondent wrote, "I thank you very much for those cards they are fine." From the collection of Ronald P. and Beatrice S. Dreese.•

A bullet • indicates that only one card has been found of a particular view.

RIGHT John C. Slear marketed a series of real photo postcards of Mifflinburg prior to 1907. This view of Chestnut Street looking east has Slear's distinctive sidebar marking complete with the credit: "Slear Photo." He used Cyko postcard stock. In this card the man noticeably silhouetted across the street from Slear's studio (on the second floor of 407 Chestnut Street) might well have been John C. Slear himself. None of Slear's other six extant cards have people in them. From the collection of Gary W. and Donna M. Slear.

Foreword

Many years ago, Foster E. Weaver, a close friend of mine, discovered a postcard album among his aunt's personal items. Fascinated by the variety of cards and the messages written on them by both family and friends, he kept the album. Ultimately, his discovery led him into the adventurous world of collecting.

Over the years, by attending flea markets, public sales, and antique shows, Foster's collection grew until over 80,000 cards had been assembled. I spent many joyful hours sorting, organizing, and filing these cards with him as well as traveling on the byways of Pennsylvania in search of more cards. We were exposed not only to real photo postcards but also to entire sets or series published by a multitude of printers. The subjects seemed endless, and the variety was amazing.

I have come to realize that the knowledge gained in this quest is priceless. What I once tolerated as silly and boring has become an integral part of my daily life. Postcard collecting introduced me to a new world of dealers and collectors as well as friendships which have lasted a decade or more.

On one of my trips to Lancaster County, Pennsylvania, I discovered a family connection to the early postcard industry. There in my hand was a real photo postcard from Union County, Pennsylvania, published and signed by my great-uncle, John C. Slear. Our family had talked about Uncle John's photography studio on Chestnut Street, Mifflinburg — its studio and darkroom areas, which were divided by a curtain; its period furnishings and large display case as well as a large gilt wall mirror for last-minute grooming. Often mentioned were his annual treks up Cemetery Hill as he lugged all the equipment needed to photograph the students at the Mifflinburg High School. But no one ever mentioned photo cards. As I shared my excitement with the dealer in front of me, I knew immediately that finding my great-uncle's postcards would become an important part of my collecting efforts. New doors were opened before me. I could touch, feel, and know actual artifacts from my family's past. People, places, and events I had heard of came to life before my very eyes.

For me, the ultimate goals of collecting have been attained: (1) to search out, sort, and assemble the best examples known to exist, continually striving to find that new acquisition and face the challenge that requires; (2) to talk to others — collectors and dealers alike — to continually research the subject and become as knowledgeable as possible. This interest led me to prepare slide shows and accept public speaking engagements. It has paved the way for me to be instrumental in helping to establish The Susquehanna Valley Postcard Club, to enlarge the postcard collection of the Union County Historical Society, and to appraise estates with postcards.

To date, helping with this book has possibly been my greatest challenge. From its inception, our goal was not only to document the photographers and their techniques but also to present a way of life that no longer exists. Although this book deals with Central Pennsylvania, it could well be interpreted as portraying rural America at the turn of the century.

Most of these cards were never before published in a book format. They bear witness to the life style contemporaneous to these pioneers in the making of "corresponding photographs."

Gary W. Slear

Past President of the Union County Historical Society and Chairman of the UCHS Archives and Museum Committee

Photographic Correspondence: Picture Postcards in Historical Context

by Jody Blake

"Don't be so tight. Write me real soon"

This message from a Union County, Pennsylvania, postcard applies as much to photo historians, who have long overlooked real photo postcards, as it does to tardy correspondents. Even at the height of their popularity in the United States, from the introduction of "private mailing cards" in 1898 to the onset of the Great Depression, real photo and other picture postcards were generally viewed with condescension. Indeed, they were thought by many to represent not only the most debased sort of written correspondence but also the crassest form of visual imagery, a reputation that has endured until the present day.[1]

According to the *Magazine of Art* (1902), postcards, which consisted of "reproductions of photographs" and "a rehash of old coloured [lithographic] scraps," were "low class from the artistic point of view" and well-suited to "an artistically low-class clientele."[2] The messages on these photographs of historic or scenic places and lithographs of comic or sentimental situations were greeted with comparable disdain. In the opinion of a contributor to *Putnam's Magazine* (1907), "to those who look for veritable communication, [the postcard is] a mockery, a flippant grin in place of real interchange of thought."[3]

During recent years there has, however, been a re-evaluation of early picture postcards among deltiologists (postcard collectors) and historians. At the center of this trend has been what is commonly referred to as the "real photo postcard." Unlike the majority of photographic postcards, which are in fact lithographic reproductions of photographs printed in ink from a plate and run through a press, the real photo postcard is an actual photograph. Because it is made directly from a negative and is exposed and developed in a darkroom, the real photo postcard is not only quite rare but also of special documentary interest.

Given the new demand for and increasing market value of real photo and other postcards, their enthusiasts are no longer looked down on by other collectors of American material culture.[4] In keeping with revisionist approaches to history, these images are also being studied by scholars more interested in the everyday experiences of ordinary people than in exceptional events and great individuals.[5] Indeed, at a time when curators and critics of visual culture are overturning the hierarchy of high versus low art, the picture postcard's anti-elitism is increasingly considered to be a virtue rather than a vice.

One indication of these changing attitudes is a growing body of publications. This literature consists primarily of surveys of pictorial postcards in general, including lithographic and photolithographic postcards, such as Richard Carline's *Pictures in the Post* (1972), Frank Staff's *The Picture Postcard and Its Origins* (1979), and Dorothy Ryan's *Picture Postcards in the United States* (1982). However, studies of real photo postcards in particular, notably Hal Morgan and Andreas Brown's *Prairie Fires and Paper Moons: The American Photographic Postcard* (1981), and Martin Parr and Jack Stasiak's *'The Actual Boot': The Photographic Post Card Boom* (1986), are now being published.[6]

This recent interest has also given rise to examinations of photographic postcards from specific localities, the most pertinent here being George Miller's *A Pennsylvania Album* (1979); by specific photographers and publishers, such as Brewster Harding's study of the Eastern Illustrating & Publishing Company of Belfast, Maine (1982), and Kim Keister's study of the Curt Teich Printing Company of Chicago (1992); or of particular subjects, such as John Baeder's *Gas, Food, and Lodging* (1982).[7]

Nevertheless, with the exception of several studies devoted to town views, especially Jay Ruby's "Images of Rural America" published in *History of Photography* (1988), the real photo postcard has not yet assumed a place alongside the other innovations that contributed to the popularization of photography. This omission from standard histories of the medium is all the more surprising given the recent questioning of accepted canons of artistic and documentary photography by scholars and practitioners alike.

Photo historians are now studying previously devalued genres. Notable among them are the nineteenth-century "carte de visite" (calling card) portrait, the equivalent of today's wallet-sized portrait; and the three-dimensional stereo view card (or stereo-

graph), the predecessor of the View-Master transparency disk.[8] Photographers have been exploring decidedly "low tech" and "low art" approaches, using "crude" equipment like toy cameras, experimenting with "primitive" non-silver processes such as the blueprint, and emulating commonplace images such as family snapshots.[9]

In this climate, photo historians are acknowledging that "old masters," such as Ansel Adams, whose Yosemite views are national icons, and Walker Evans, renowned for his images of American vernacular architecture, actually admired or even made postcards. Contemporary photographers have been electing to send their own landscapes and cityscapes through the mail with handwritten messages and postage stamps on the back.[10] It is time, therefore, for what a Union County studio called "corresponding photographs"[11] to enter the history of photography.

Postcards for Fun or Profit

In 1910, a dollar would buy a bag of groceries as well as a dozen picture postcards, and even the least expensive Kodak camera (around $5) cost the equivalent of an industrial worker's weekly wages. Thus, the ability to purchase or to make real photo postcards was hardly within the reach of every American.[12] Nevertheless, a notable aspect of the photo postcard phenomenon, at least at its onset in the decade preceding World War I, was the decentralization of the production and marketing of these images and their resultant accessibility to small-town and big-city dwellers alike.

In Union County, as in rural areas throughout the country, there was a wide range of photographers and publishers eager to take advantage of the vogue for sending and collecting pictorial postcards. There was a stiff competition between local photographers and outsiders, especially the publishers of color or black-and-white photolithographic postcards, who were accused by *American Amateur Photographer* (1906) of flooding markets with cheap mass-produced images.[13] In addition, there was considerable rivalry between professional photographers and hobbyists, who were regarded as "business spoilers" by *Abel's Photographic Weekly* (1909) because of their homemade portraits and views.[14]

This variety of picture postcard makers resulted in diversity of photographic and photo-mechanical

---

A postcard display rack at a souvenir stand and a banner advertising postcards at Lindig's Art Store, 326 Market Street, Lewisburg, provide evidence of the retailing of postcards in the decade before World War I. The view of the north side of the 300 block of Market Street has an embossed stamp on the front "LEWISBURG, PENNA." and is attributed to Edwin S. Heiser. Both cards were made as early as 1907. From the collections of Gary W. and Donna M. Slear, and Janice C. Dreese. ••

printing techniques as well as of subject matter and stylistic approaches. Especially marketable views, including local landmarks of topical interest or scenic spots lending themselves to artistic treatment, were issued virtually simultaneously in a variety of processes. Real photo postcards, made by local professionals and amateurs, included blue prints (cyanotypes) and sepia prints as well as standard black-and-white silver prints. Photolithographic postcards were published by commercial firms either in black and white or in color, using up to four different inks. The printers of these photolithographic postcards sometimes took liberties with the original photo by removing unsightly or outdated elements or by inserting dramatic elements such as clouds and a moon.[15]

National or regional publishers were responsible for the majority of the photolithographic "souvenir postcards" that filled the rotating racks and vending machines in the tourist kiosks, postcard shops, and newspaper stands of Central Pennsylvania. Particularly active in the towns of this area were the Albertype Company, the Rotograph Company, and the Souvenir Post Card Company, all of the New York City area. Like their counterparts throughout the country, these

---

This view of the Lewisburg Bridge exists both as a real photo postcard and as a color photolithographic postcard. Prior to the 1940s and 1950s, when publishers began using color film, colored postcards were actually photolithographs. Detailed instructions were provided to the printer along with the original black and white image, making the colors reproduced on these photolithographic postcards fairly accurate. Here, the lithographer added a moon and clouds and printed the card in blue, yellow and red ink to transform a straightforward view of the Lewisburg Bridge into a romantic nighttime scene. The color photolithographic card was printed in Germany and postmarked September 16, 1908, two months after the opening of the bridge. From the collections of the Union County Historical Society #84.13.1 and Gary W. and Donna M. Slear.

firms had their cards photomechanically reproduced from negatives or prints made by company photographers or purchased from local photographers.[16]

Local retailers in Union County, as elsewhere, however, also functioned as publishers of photolithographic as well as real photo postcards. These "souvenir views" were especially appealing to merchants who were already in the art or stationery business, including Lindig's Art Store of Lewisburg and Roy Hartman's Stationery of Mifflinburg. Postcards were also a potentially lucrative sideline for general merchants, such as F. H. Maurer's General Store of New Berlin and G. D. Gast and Son's Department Store of Mifflinburg. According to the *Dry Goods Economist* (1905), "[Illustrated postal cards] have long passed the fad stage and appear to have become a permanent feature. The line is a good one for the retailer because of the small amount of space necessary to make a fair showing of them and, further, because they bear a good profit."[17]

Whether published locally, by regional or national firms, these commercial view postcards were printed for the most part in Germany, which until World War

This photograph of Buffalo Creek, Lewisburg, was made into a real photo postcard, using the cyanotype process, as well as into a color photolithographic postcard. The cyanotype (also known as a ferroprussiate print because it is sensitized with iron salts) was popular among the makers of real photo postcards. It yielded a distinctive blue print with a narrow tonal range that was especially suited to landscapes. Moreover, as was pointed out by *Camera and Darkroom*, January 1904, the cyanotype was an extremely simple process, because "a thorough washing is all that is needed to complete the picture after it has been printed. With other sensitizing solutions some chemical method of fixation is usually required." The cyanotype is postmarked 1906, and the color photolithograph, published by Lindig's Art Studio, is postmarked 1909. From the collections of the Union County Historical Society #92.9.91.75 and Gary W. and Donna M. Slear.

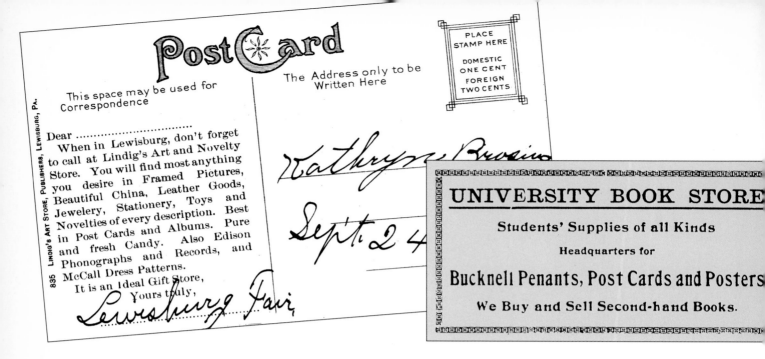

I was the leader in the field of black-and-white and four-color photolithography. Printers in Belgium and other European countries as well as in U.S. cities, including Chicago, New York, and Philadelphia, however, competed for their share of the postcard business by means of sales agents and direct advertising. A typical advertisement, published in *Photographic Journal of America* (1915), announced, "Local Views/ 440 Broadway/New York/Postcards printed to order from 100 up in black and colors — ten styles. Buildings, interiors, churches, street scenes, etc. 500% profit."[18]

The real photo postcard, encompassing portraiture, advertising, and reportage as well as view photography, was primarily the domain of local professionals. In the larger towns of Union County, these consisted of studio-based photographers, such as Fred W. Lindig of Lewisburg, John C. Slear of Mifflinburg, and John D. Swanger and Arthur R. Ishiguro of Milton. These studio photographers were joined by entrepreneurs, notably William "Grover" Bierly of Mifflinburg, Urs H. Eisenhauer of Millmont, Stephen B. Horton of West Milton, and Maurice E. Royer of Mifflinburg, for whom the making of real photo postcards was an important if short-lived venture in which they engaged while continuing to practice other trades.

Studio portraits were a significant component of the postcard phenomenon. With the exception of the fact that they were printed on postcard stock, these differed little in terms of poses, settings, and lighting from "cabinet cards" and other types of studio portraits available at the time. There was concern, therefore, expressed in professional journals, such as *Abel's Photographic Weekly* (1909), that the fad for portrait postcards, which generally cost a dollar or less for a dozen, would divert customers from higher-priced formats which were determined by size, paper, finish, or mounting.[19]

Misgivings concerning postcard portraiture are understandable in light of efforts by studio photographers, such as John C. Slear of Slear's Studio in Mifflinburg, to maintain a reputation and a clientele for high-quality portrait work. In an advertisement published in the *Mifflinburg Telegraph* (1907), for example, Slear stated, "There are fads of cheap Photographs, but our ambition has been above making Photographs so cheap that it necessitates a sacrifice in quality."[20]

For the most part, postcard portraits were regarded as a stimulus to business. An attention-getting novelty, they encouraged return visits to the local photographer. They were also ideal for holiday and other gift-giving occasions promoted by studios.[21] This was apparently the point of view of the Lindig Art Studio of Lewisburg, whose photographer at the time was Ellen H. Shields. In circulars from about 1908 this studio not only advertised portrait enlargements but also promoted "The Newest Fad. Souvenir Post Cards. Have your photograph made on a post-card."

Recording scenes and documenting events were also an integral part of professional photographic

---

Postcard publishers, such as Lindig's Art Store and the University Book Store, Lewisburg, relied on direct advertisement. Lindig sent out postcards to inform customers that he would have a display at the 1908 Lewisburg Fair, and the University Book Store purchased space in the Bucknell University newspaper, *Orange and Blue*, October 10, 1908, to publicize its school souvenirs. The postcard is from the collection of Gary W. and Donna M. Slear.

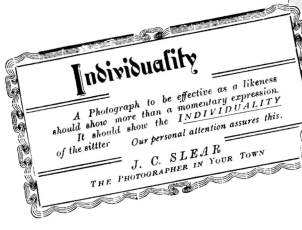

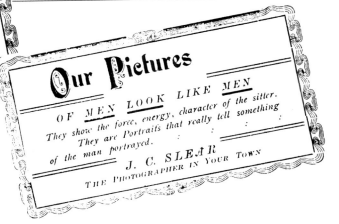

In the early twentieth century, studio photographers continued to offer standard formats, including "cabinet portraits" such as this portrait of the twins Anna Ellen Slear and Albert Ernest Slear, made by their uncle, John C. Slear, of Mifflinburg, c. 1919. Many studios also promoted "corresponding photographs" printed on postcard stock, such as this portrait of Harry Morton Billmeyer and Helen Geraldine Young Billmeyer, taken at the time of their wedding in 1927 by Arthur R. Ishiguro of Milton. From the collections of Gary W. and Donna M. Slear, and Ruth Anna Billmeyer Zimmermann.

Advertisements for John C. Slear, published in the *Mifflinburg Telegraph,* February 6, 1914, and March 6, 1914, and the Lindig Art Studio, c. 1908, are indicative of stiff competition among portrait photographers in the era of real photo postcards. According to *Abel's Photographic Weekly*, February 6, 1909, "It does not pay to demand more than the customer can pay, but it does pay to give and to persuade the customer to take the very best grade that he or she can afford. If the postcard is worked shrewdly it is a fine thing. If it is not worked shrewdly it can become a great nuisance." The Lindig advertisement is from the collection of John Van Buskirk.

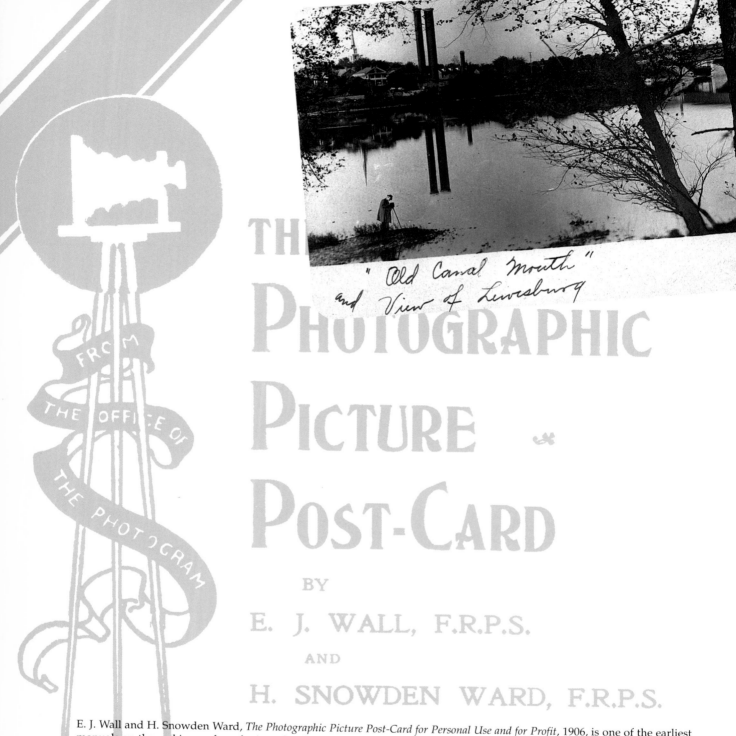

"Old Canal Mouth"
and View of Lewisburg

THE PHOTOGRAPHIC PICTURE POST-CARD

BY

E. J. WALL, F.R.P.S.

AND

H. SNOWDEN WARD, F.R.P.S.

E. J. Wall and H. Snowden Ward, *The Photographic Picture Post-Card for Personal Use and for Profit*, 1906, is one of the earliest manuals on the making and marketing of real photo postcards. It contains chapters on photographic equipment, darkroom techniques, and publishing strategies. Photograph courtesy of the George Eastman House.

A photographer is shown at work with a tripod-mounted camera near the "Old Canal Mouth, Lewisburg." This view was made prior to 1907 by Edwin S. Heiser and may be a self-portrait of this prolific maker of real photo postcards. From the collection of the Union County Historical Society #92.9.91.61.

These cyanotypes are among the nighttime snow scenes that Nelson F. Davis made on University Avenue, Lewisburg, near the entrance to Bucknell University. The first photograph (which was also made into a black-and-white photolithographic card titled "Winter Scene, University Ave. at Night, Lewisburg, Pa.") was reportedly made using a large aperture lens from 11 p.m. to 1 a.m. Because of this two-hour exposure, pedestrians were able to pass in front of Davis' camera without leaving any trace on the negative. Davis most likely created the illusion of falling snow in the second photograph by spotting the negative (or a sheet of glass placed over the negative) with ink, which created white spots on the final print. Both postcards were postmarked 1906. From the collection of the Union County Historical Society #92.9.91.69 and #92.9.91.70.

LONDON

DAWBARN & WARD, LTD.

practice in the early twentieth century. This was especially the case in rural areas where commercial and press photography, as opposed to portraiture, were only beginning to emerge as specialties.[22] According to "A Small-Town Photographer," who shared his experiences in *Abel's Photographic Weekly* (1909), "If I sat down in my gallery and waited for trade, I should grow slim. . . . I guess that not much more than half my work is straightforward studio work."[23]

The making of view postcards was, therefore, a logical extension of the activities of professional photographers in Central Pennsylvania and other rural areas. Real photo postcards provided them with a new market for their work, especially in the less populous parts of Union County, where there are only isolated examples of commercial photolithographic view cards.[24] This was the optimistic opinion of John A. Tennant, editor of *Photo-Miniature*, whose special issue on real photo postcards (1908) was one of the first practical manuals on the subject. According to Tennant, "The photographic post-card offers possibilities of profit even to the individual worker with limited facilities, for there is always a market for cards of special or local interest, in circumstances where the commercial post-card does not enter or can have no place."[25]

Professional photographers, however, were not the only ones who explored the potential of real photo postcards. Skilled amateurs, eager to gain recognition for their work and to supplement their income (or at least to defray the costs of their expensive hobby), also

marketed real photo postcards. In an article on "Amateur Photography that Pays" in *Camera and Darkroom* (1903), M. D. S. Hymers advised concerning postcards, "Print them with the choicest views from your home town (or any other with which you are familiar) and invite the tourist public to buy."[26]

Union County amateurs, including Eli R. Bartoo and Nelson F. Davis, who were affiliated with Bucknell University, heeded this advice. Like Bartoo, an undergraduate student who was reportedly working his way through college in this manner, they sold their real photo view postcards independently. Or, as was the case with Davis, a biology professor who photographed scenes around Lewisburg as well as on the Bucknell campus, they marketed especially salable images through local merchants, such as Lindig's Art Store.

Casual snapshooters as well as serious hobbyists embraced this novel way to share photographs with family and friends.[27] The popularization of the real photo postcard occurred a decade after the introduction in 1888 of the first Kodak cameras. Relatively cheap and easy to use, Kodaks made photography

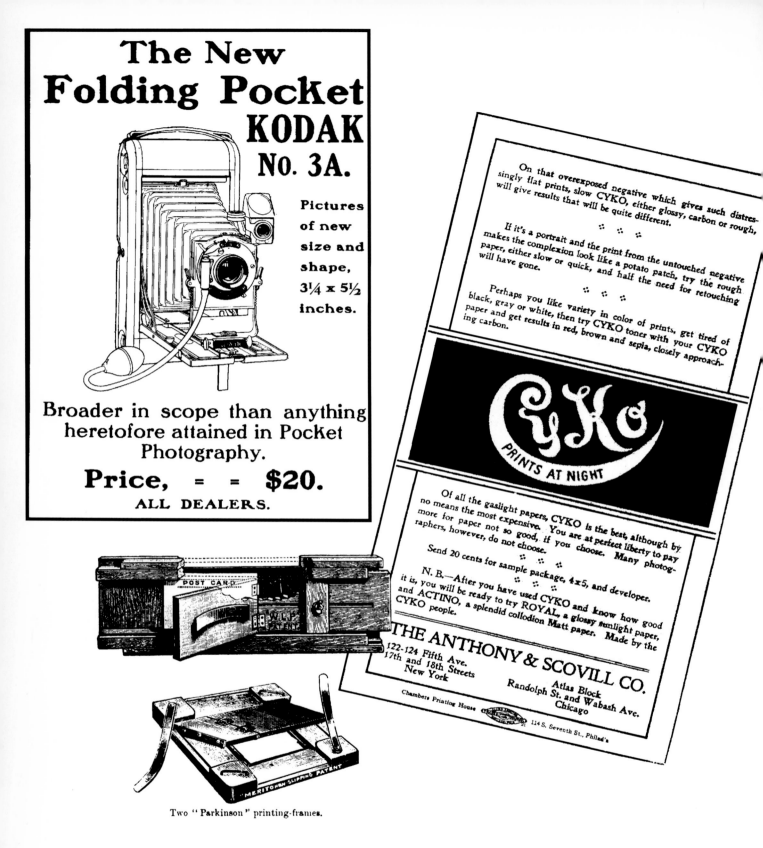

The New Folding Pocket KODAK No. 3A.

Pictures of new size and shape, 3¼ x 5½ inches.

Broader in scope than anything heretofore attained in Pocket Photography.

Price, = = $20.
ALL DEALERS.

Two "Parkinson" printing-frames.

On that overexposed negative which gives such distressingly flat prints, slow CYKO, either glossy, carbon or rough, will give results that will be quite different.

If it's a portrait and the print from the untouched negative makes the complexion look like a potato patch, try the rough paper, either slow or quick, and half the need for retouching will have gone.

Perhaps you like variety in color of prints, get tired of black, gray or white, then try CYKO toners with your CYKO paper and get results in red, brown and sepia, closely approaching carbon.

CyKo
PRINTS AT NIGHT

Of all the gaslight papers, CYKO is the best, although by no means the most expensive. You are at perfect liberty to pay more for paper not so good, if you choose. Many photographers, however, do not choose.

Send 20 cents for sample package, 4x5, and developer.

N. B.—After you have used CYKO and know how good it is, you will be ready to try ROYAL, a glossy sunlight paper, and ACTINO, a splendid collodion Matt paper. Made by the CYKO people.

THE ANTHONY & SCOVILL CO.
122-124 Fifth Ave.
17th and 18th Streets
New York

Atlas Block
Randolph St. and Wabash Ave.
Chicago

Chambers Printing House   114 S. Seventh St., Philad's

Among the products designed for the making of real photo postcards were: "The New Folding Pocket Kodak No. 3A," advertised in *Camera*, December 1903; "Parkinson Printing Frames," illustrated in Wall and Ward, *The Photographic Picture Post-Card*, 1906; "Cyko Prints at Night," advertised in *Camera*, May 1903; "Velox Post Cards," advertised in *Camera*, January 1904; and "Velox Transparent Water Color Stamps" advertised in *The American Photographic Weekly*, 1915. Photographs courtesy of the Kansas State Historical Society and George Eastman House.

A touch of nature with every stroke of the brush if you color your landscapes with

VELOX TRANSPARENT WATER COLOR STAMPS

Blue skies, green fields, red sunsets—the beautiful color combinations of nature are artistically, easily, and simply reproduced.

No knowledge of art is necessary—the colors are self-blending and the book of instructions accompanying each set of colors, takes the place of experience.

THE PRICE.

Book of Velox Water Color Stamps (12 colors), - - - - - - - - $ .25
Complete Velox Water Color Outfit, including book of color stamps, three brushes and palette, - - - - - - - - - - .75

EASTMAN KODAK COMPANY,
ROCHESTER, N. Y.

your dealer's.

Photographic Post-Cards.

By Chas. E. Fairman.

THE use of the souvenir post-card has become almost universal. Not only is the post-card used as a medium for sending brief messages, such as may with safety be read by the curious through whose hands the message may chance to pass, but in a majority of instances the post-card seems designed for purely advertising purposes, for the exploitation of the charms of summer resorts and sea-side attractions, until the message is but a secondary consideration, and the selection of post-cards containing pretty pictures—which shall be treasured as souvenirs by the person receiving these brief records of the places visited by the tourist—has become a custom which is growing in popularity as the seasons pass.

In some localities the revenue derived from the use of post-cards during some seasons of the year far exceeds the revenue received from the sale of stamps for letters, and to such an extent is this sending of souvenir cards practiced that the Post Office Department has adopted very liberal rules, and almost

CHAS. E. FAIRMAN

EXAMPLES OF AMATEUR POSTAL CARD WORK

Charles E. Fairman, "Photographic Post-cards," *Camera and Darkroom*, January 1904, was among the instructional articles addressed primarily to amateur photographers.

accessible to individuals without the means to acquire expensive camera and darkroom equipment, the inclination to calculate apertures and exposures, or the desire to become adept at developing and printing glass plate negatives.[28]

Making Corresponding Photographs

Instructions for making real photo postcards, including advice on subjects and marketing tips as well as technical information, were readily available to amateurs and professionals alike. Journals such as *Camera and Darkroom* and *American Amateur Photographer* included instructional articles for their readers. Book-length pamphlets were also published, including *The Photographic Picture Post-Card* (1906), written by E. J. Wall and H. Snowden Ward, members of the Royal Photographic Society of Britain; and John A. Tennant, ed., "Photographic Post-Card" (1908), a special issue of *Photo-Miniature*.[29]

Local photographers used the backs of postcards as their own forum for discussing the technical challenges posed by this new photographic format. They addressed topics ranging from the difficulties of posing, such as eyes squinting in the sunlight and animals that refused to stay still;[30] to basic camera operations, including focusing;[31] as well as standard darkroom procedures, such as exposing and fixing prints;[32] and even special technical matters, such as the use of a magnesium flash.[33] Messages such as these are a reminder of a period when, especially among newcomers to photography, achieving a successful image was not necessarily a routine occurrence. Moreover, as these comments attest, the making of photographs was still remarkable enough to be considered news in its own right.

The real photo postcard utilized existing equipment, supplies, and processes. Nevertheless, its success depended on the photographic industry's development of products designed for this format. Postcard photos could be made with virtually any camera, from the most sophisticated to the simplest. The professional's tripod-mounted view camera, for example, permitted viewing the scene to be photographed and utilized glass plate negatives. In contrast, the amateur's handheld box camera was merely pointed at the subject to be taken and was loaded with celluloid roll film. Special cameras were, however, designed to produce negatives corresponding to the standard postcard dimensions of 3¼" x 5½."[34] These included the professional Graflex postcard camera (1907) and the Conley folding plate camera (c. 1900-1910), as well as the amateur No. 3A Folding Pocket Kodak Camera (1903) and the Weno Hawk Eye (1906).[35]

Professional and lay photographers could chose to prepare their own card stock, coating and sensitizing it using standard chemical formulas, then applying the "post card" designation on the back with a printing press or a rubber stamp. A wide array of presensitized and preprinted postcards for use in professional studios and amateur darkrooms were also available. So-called gaslight developing cards included Kodak's *Velox* (1902) and *Azo* (1904), Ansco's *Cyko*, and Defender's *Argo*, trademarks familiar from the "place stamp here" box on the backs of real photo postcards. These gelatin silver chloride papers were exposed beneath the negative in artificial light and then developed and fixed with chemicals to bring out and stabilize the image. Various daylight printing-out, self-toning, and non-silver cards, which yielded a visible image on exposure to sunlight or resulted in "colored" prints, were also used. The most popular of these alternative processes among amateurs was the cyanotype or blueprint, which was easy to sensitize and required no chemical fixing.[36]

Special printers designed for exposing real photo postcards were also available. High-speed, large-volume printing machines, which held stacks or rolls of sensitized paper and made hundreds of postcards from the same negative per hour, facilitated their commercial mass production. Small-town producers of real photo postcards, for whom such a level of automation was not feasible, may have contracted their printing out to larger companies. In addition, printing machines and frames that could be adjusted to produce real photo postcards in smaller quantities and at lesser speeds were also marketed and may have been used by local photographers and studios. Kodak also marketed amateur printing boxes that accommodated negatives and paper for this popular format. However, many snapshooters, seduced by George Eastman's slogan, "You push the button, we do the rest," elected to have their film printed as postcards by professionals.[37]

Photography journals and books were filled with paid ads for these and other products, which, in the manner of today's infomercials, could be confused with articles. Kodak engaged in such advertising with the business savvy for which it was famous.[38] In *Photo-Miniature* (1914), for example, Kodak suggested to customers, "Since the Kodak Film Tank has eliminated the darkroom, and you can develop your vacation films wherever you may happen to be, it has come to be a common thing for the amateur to finish his vacation pictures on the spot and to send Velox Post-Cards, from his own negatives, to the folks at home."[39] As this ad indicates, Kodak aggressively promoted what amounted to a "total package" for postcard making,

as the "how-to" publications of the period pointed out, transforming a good negative into a successful postcard involved specific considerations and required particular techniques.

Photographers, for example, experimented with various approaches to composing the fronts of real photo postcards. When using a negative larger than the dimensions of the postcard, they frequently printed the photograph from edge to edge. To give the postcard a more finished look, they masked the negative with opaque black paper to produce a narrow white border around the photograph. When the negative was smaller than 3¼" x 5½," masking was necessary to avoid the unsightly ragged or black edges that appear on some cards. The white border could also be used to provide space for a message at the bottom or the side of the photograph. Moreover, when cut into a special shape, the mask became a pictorial element,

including camera and film, developing tank and chemicals, printing box and masks, various grades of paper, and even water colors and paint brushes for hand tinting.[40]

Marketing strategies such as this enabled Kodak to sell its cameras relatively inexpensively, confident that it would make a profit on accessories and supplies. This promotion of amateur photography culminated in the pages of *Kodakery*, first published in 1913, which was essentially an advertisement for the types of camera and darkroom products that were for sale at local retailers, such as Edwin S. Heiser's drugstore in Lewisburg, as well as at photography studios. In an ad in the *Lewisburg Chronicle* (1909), for example, The Swanger Studio of Milton announced that it sold "kodacs [sic], amateur supplies, art goods, modern equipment."

Thus equipped, professionals and amateurs tackled the challenges of printing real photo postcards. This involved routine darkroom techniques, such as making contact prints from entire negatives or printing enlargements of portions of negatives. Nevertheless,

enhancing the meaning of a view or a portrait, or simply asserting, in the manner of the trompe l'oeil frames used on some photolithographic postcards, its status as a picture.

Most professional photographers chose to add identifying titles (as well as signatures) to their cards.

These glass gelatine dry plate negatives were exposed by Nelson F. Davis, c. 1900-1910, whose photographs appeared, although without credit, on postcards of Bucknell University and Lewisburg. From the University Archives, Ellen Clarke Bertrand Library, Bucknell University.

The Eastman Kodak 3A Developing and Printing Outfit, first marketed in 1911, contained everything needed to develop and print real photo postcards. Included were developing trays and a printing frame, shown here, as well as a candle lamp, a graduate, a stirring rod, developing and fixing powders, and two dozen sheets of Velox paper. From the collection of Chandler Blackington.

Opaque paper masks, either commercially produced or custom-made, were used to create the decorative frames around these views of Spring Garden and Mazeppa, made in 1907 or later. In the opinion of *Photo-Miniature*, October 1908, "The individual worker can give his post-cards a note of distinctiveness and character by …the use of mats giving a simple, but tasteful, decorative design. In fact, once we depart from the commercial method of printing views in full size on the post-card, we have an extensive and interesting field for the expression of individual taste and fancy." From the collections of Ronald Nornhold and Gary W. and Donna M. Slear. • •

The easiest way to do this was, of course, on the finished card itself, using pen and ink or a rubber stamp. When multiple copies were desired, it was more efficient to incorporate the title into the negative itself. This could be done by hand, using pen and India ink, and writing in reverse on the film itself, which was sometimes stripped of its emulsion to provide a black background for the white lettering. To avoid the difficulties of reversing letters and writing from right to left (which occasionally resulted in errors), one could write the title on a piece of celluloid or other transparent material affixed face down on the negative. Reverse type lettering kits such as "Titleit" and "Nameit" were also available and used by some photographers to label the subjects of their

real photo postcards.[41]

Choosing Subjects that Sell

The prevailing wisdom, expressed in booklets and articles devoted to photo postcards, was that there was a relationship between the producers (whether commercial, professional or amateur), their audiences, and the resultant images. Although by no means rigid, these distinctions are a helpful analytical tool. If one examines postcards of a typical rural locality, the types of subjects and interpretations do correspond to those identified by Tennant, Wall and Ward, and others in their guides to postcard-making. Likewise, there is a general correlation between the imagery of commercial, professional and amateur cards and the categories

Stephen B. Horton stripped the emulsion from the negative to create a black background for the hand lettering on this postcard of the school house, Mazeppa, postmarked 1910. The slight leftward slant of the letters provides telltale evidence that the title was written by hand, in reverse and from right to left, on the negative. Maurice E. Royer used a reverse type kit to create the bold block lettering on this postcard of the Mifflinburg Body and Gear plant, postmarked 1914. • The number following the title is typical of those which photographers used to catalog their negatives and prints. From the collections of the Union County Historical Society #92.9.89.37 and Gary W. and Donna M. Slear.

William "Grover" Bierly took this "Birds Eye View" of Mifflinburg from Cemetery Hill on the south edge of town in 1914. In the era of early aviation, photography from airships (dirigibles) and airplanes was becoming a reality. Although there are occasional aerial views of Central Pennsylvania, local photographers continued to rely upon natural and architectural overlooks for their postcard views. As one publisher noted on a photolithographic card of Lewisburg, "[This is] as near a bird's eye view as is possible without the use of an air ship." From the collection of the Union County Historical Society #85.7.6.

proposed by these writers of the period.

General views of a town were the mainstay of postcards, whether these were commercially published photolithographs or professionally produced real photos. Union County postcards, like those from other areas, routinely featured views of towns taken from overlooking hills or from the vantage point of pedestrians on the main street.[42] Although these town views had a greater potential for sales, they presented a superficial picture of the area and its inhabitants. According to Wall and Ward, authors of *The Photographic Picture Post-Card* (1906), "the most common fault in local view cards [of entire valleys or of villages] is that they embrace too much and do not emphasize the important points."[43]

The creation of more particularized views, however, was considered to be the province of local professionals and skilled amateurs. According to Tennant of *Photo-Miniature* (1908), "The vital thing is to select subjects which are not hackneyed or overdone; to get something which cannot be had in the shops or seen

opinion of Tennant, who advised photographers to avoid the views made by commercial publishers, "whose photographer spent half a day in the village or about town," and to concentrate on "the other views which we ourselves know through repeated walks and visits."[46]

Likewise, they were encouraged to exploit their ability to record these sites in a variety of seasons and weather conditions, for example "at sundown with sky effects" or "under a covering of snow."[47] According to Wall and Ward, "The seasons offer a theme, and any particular favorite spot, in Spring, Summer, Autumn and Winter, may have a profitable popularity. A good series of snow scenes is almost certain of success."[48] Central Pennsylvania photographers took such recommendations to heart, resulting in snow scenes and twilight views by Nelson F. Davis, Nelson A. Caulkins, and Edwin S. Heiser, all photographs that are technical tours de force.[49]

In addition, it was recommended that local photographers experiment with special photographic tech-

at the news-stand photo display."[44] A contributor to *American Amateur Photographer* (1906) agreed when he stated, "Seeing, then, that the photographic picture postcard cannot compete with the mechanical . . . it remains only to give the photographs a personal or local interest."[45]

Local photographers were urged, therefore, to take advantage of their knowledge of a town's byways, such as the "trysting stile" or the "brook and its winding path," as well as of its thoroughfares. This was the

niques, such as the making of composite images. Many a postcard view of a church or a house was given added human interest by the insertion of a portrait of the local pastor or the famous owner. By combining a group of views from a given locality on a single postcard, photographers also created images that could truly stand for a town such as Lewisburg or White Deer.[50]

Local photographers were also expected to record private homes and their residents as well as public

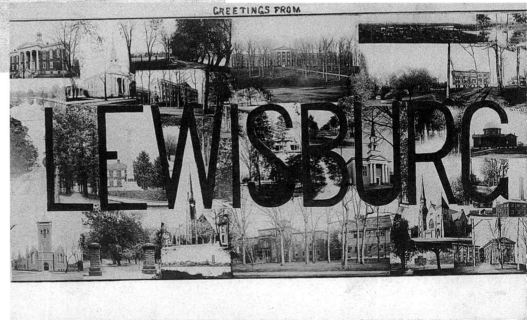

These postcards, the one commemorating the fiftieth anniversary of the United Evangelical Church, Winfield, founded 1856, and the other extending "Greetings from Lewisburg," made before 1907, are photographic composites. The combination printing of negatives was among the special "treatments" recommended in "how-to" publications. *Photo-Miniature*, October 1908, noted that "A very attractive and satisfactory post-card for many uses, and one which has the desirable note of difference from the average commercial card, is the composite post-card. . . . It may include a series of views in and about a suburban or town house, a favorite church, the public buildings of the city." From the collections of Ronald Nornhold and the Union County Historical Society #92.9.91.1. ••

Because photographic emulsions were unusually sensitive to blue, resulting in overexposure, photographing skies and clouds presented a special challenge for early twentieth-century photographers. Nelson A. Caulkins, in his postcard of the Watsontown-White Deer Ferry made in 1907 or later, and Edwin S. Heiser, in his postcard of the Susquehanna at Lewisburg made prior to 1907, solved this problem by taking their dramatic photographs of cloudy skies in the evening. From the collections of the Union County Historical Society #82.2.32• and Gary W. and Donna M. Slear.

monuments and luminaries. Consequently, house views were an important field for the makers of real photo postcards. Undoubtedly, many of these photographs were commissioned. Journals also advised photographers to make postcards of residences "on speculation," a strategy employed by Union County photographers, including Urs H. Eisenhauer. According to *American Amateur Photographer* (1906), "Samples sent [of homes] should be accompanied by a card or circular saying that copies could be had at so much per dozen, and especially that none should be sold without the permission of the party represented."[51]

Real photo postcards also made portraiture avail-

able to rural residents for whom studio visits were out of reach geographically or financially. Recognizing, in the words of a contributor to *Camera and Darkroom* (1903), that farmers were as eager for portraits as "city belles" and "city beaus,"[52] photographers in Central Pennsylvania took to the road. Unlike studio photographers with their skylights, they photographed out-of-doors at the homes of their clients. However, by means of improvised backdrops and ground coverings, such as rugs or even quilts, they sought to replicate the expected fixtures as well as the standard poses of a portrait studio. In this way, they approximated the formality expected in a period when having

Urs H. Eisenhauer was among the photographers who exploited the market for house portraits. On this postcard of a Lewisburg farmhouse he wrote, "I thought I would send you your Home on a Post Card if you want any more send 60¢ and i will send you a doz of them." Postmarked Millmont, February 9, 1910, this card was sent to Mr. O. C. Eisenhauer, Lewisburg. One of his satisfied customers noted on this postcard of her Millmont home that "Mr. Eisenhauer took our house the other day, and you shall have one. When you come to see us once you will not miss the place." Postmarked Millmont, September 24, 1909, this card was sent to Miss Nellie Smith, Washington, D. C. From the collections of Gary W. and Donna M. Slear, and the Union County Historical Society #90.21.10. ● ●

Union County residents who posed for real photo postcard portraits included: the Lewis and Catherine Speese family of Millmont, photographed by their neighbor, Urs H. Eisenhauer, c. 1909; a family from western Union County attributed to Eisenhauer, 1907 or later; and the Winter Sisters of New Berlin, 1907. Although these photographs were made out-of-doors at the homes of their subjects, the poses and props imitate those of formal studio portraiture. From the collections of Delphia Shirk, Richard D. and Leah Bingaman, and Gary W. and Donna M. Slear. ● ● ●

Mary Barber Hagey made these postcard "snapshots" of her children and their friends in the 1920s. Photographed near the Hagey residence in White Deer, these postcards show: Dorothy Hagey, preparing to throw a snowball in front of the White Deer Bridge; and the Bergenstock, Fisher, Hagey, Hursh, and Koch children cooling off in the White Deer Creek. From the collection of Betty Hagey Herald.••

Engraving of Lewisburg from Earl Shinn, *Picturesque Glimpses of Philadelphia and Pennsylvania*, 1875. From Special Collections, Ellen Clarke Bertrand Library, Bucknell University.

one's picture taken was still a ritualized event.

Finally, amateurs' postcards were distinguished from the others on the basis of the "semi-intimate interest shown in the choice of subjects."[53] As was the case with snapshot photography in general, subjects were selected from the realm of house or garden and included familiar figures in characteristic activities. In addition, given the personal connection between photographer and sitter, and the unobtrusive character of snapshot cameras, these images are often characterized by intimacy and spontaneity. In the words of a contributor to *Camera and Darkroom* (1904), "It will be found that the absent friends who receive these little souvenirs of places or faces, will feel a much greater satisfaction because of the fact that the work has in it a personal character."[54]

Typical in this respect are the real photo postcards by Mary Elizabeth Barber Hagey. These were made in the 1920s outside the White Deer residence that she shared with her husband Fred and their three children. Formerly an "accommodation house" or inn, this structure also contained the family's general store. Located on "the square" with its post office and adjacent to the creek with its "iron bridge," the Hagey home was at the center of activity in White Deer. In a period when "children were allowed to be children" and extended families were the rule rather than the exception, the Hagey home was the site of outdoor play by Dorothy, William, and Betty Hagey as well as the multi-generational gatherings of the Eberharts, Barbers, and Hageys. Mary Hagey recorded these events, using a folding Kodak camera, in real photo postcards that exemplify the often impromptu posing and the domestic subjects of amateur snapshots.[55]

"I suppose you will recognize this place"
The "X" marking the spot of one's home or business, or the arrow indicating one's presence in a street scene or at a parade are considered blemishes by most postcard collectors. As is the case with identifications and inquiries, such as "this is the path I trod many times" and "can you recognize the guy in the window?", these defacements are actually invaluable evidence of the importance of postcards as personal documents as well as tourist souvenirs.

For the inhabitants of rural America, postcards were especially important in creating a sense of community identity.[56] The citizens of Philadelphia to the east or Pittsburgh to the west were accustomed to seeing their cities pictured in the graphically and photographically illustrated publications of the period, as well as in photographic views and stereographs. This was not the case, however, for the residents of the more than a dozen communities in Union County,

from Spring Garden and White Deer in the north, to Glen Iron and Laurelton in the west, and New Berlin and Winfield in the south.

Indeed, even when major towns were mentioned in books, they were not necessarily illustrated. Lewisburg, the county seat, and its "neat sparkling houses, its shaded streets, and its busy aspect" were described in Eli Bowen's *Pictorial Sketchbook of Pennsylvania* (1854). It was not pictured, however, in the 500 detailed engravings of towns, industries, and railroads in this informational guidebook.[57] This "busy little retreat of learning" "pleasantly situated on the west bank of the river" fared better in Earl Shinn's *Picturesque Glimpses of Philadelphia and Pennsylvania* (1875). Here, three vignettes, of the Susquehanna River, Market Street and the University at Lewisburg (Bucknell University), were devoted to Lewisburg, its natural setting and architectural landmarks.[58]

In the later nineteenth and early twentieth centuries, the larger towns of Union County were also occasionally documented in stereo view cards. Consisting of

Stereograph of floodwaters at Market Street near Sixth Street, Lewisburg, by J. Wesley Cornelius, 1889. J. C. Gundy's stove and tinware store is on the right. From the collection of the Union County Historical Society #92.9.33.

Photo tradecard for J. C. Gundy, Lewisburg, c. 1889; and real photo postcard of Miller's Barber Shop, Laurelton, by Stephen B. Horton, postmarked 1910.• From the collection of the Union County Historical Society #92.9.88.29 and #92.9.89.11.

two photographs of a scene, usually made with a special double-lens camera, these yielded a three-dimensional effect when viewed through a hand-held or table-mounted stereoscope. Real photo stereographs were produced by area photographers such as J. Wesley Cornelius of Lewisburg, who in the 1880s marketed "choice stereopic gems" of the town. Stereographs of Union County were, however, relatively rare at a time when most Americans turned to the parlor stereoscope for educational views of distant places and entertaining images of narrative tableaux.

Significantly, therefore, it was in terms of civic pride that commentators explained the growth of town view postcards. Indeed, according to *American Illustrated Magazine* (1906), the driving force behind the fad was "pangs of jealousy" on the part of the citizens of rival towns who were eager to have "postal cards which set forth the glories of their native place."[59] Consequently, in the opinion of a contributor to *Camera and Darkroom* (1903), the photographer who portrayed his own town on postcards would be regarded as a "local benefactor" in the eyes of its residents, who would "be glad to advertise their progressive town in this way."[60]

Makers of real photo postcards did, in fact, serve as promoters for small towns as well as reporters of their newsworthy events. In the late nineteenth century, photography began replacing other graphic media in publicizing business and industry. Large companies, such as General Electric and Sears, Roebuck and Co., who were pioneers in this aspect of public relations, maintained their own photographic staffs. Smaller firms, such as the flour mills, iron foundries, buggy works, stores, hotels, and barbershops of rural America, however, had to rely on local professionals. So, in regions in which businesses and industries were among the major landmarks, postcards were simultaneously "souvenir views" and "publicity shots." Like the engraved, lithographic, or occasionally photographic trade cards that preceded them, postcards were an inexpensive means of direct advertising.[61] Sent to business associates or distributed to private customers, these photographs were highly effective in promoting businesses and industries as well as their products and services.

At this time, halftone reproductions of photographs were assuming an increasingly important place in the urban press. By 1905 half of the illustrations in New York City's newspapers were photographic, and by the 1920s almost all of them were.[62] This trend was summed up by John Everard in *Photographs for the Papers: How to Take and Place Them* (1914; 2nd ed. 1923), a "how-to" book directed at British photographers. According to Everard, "Readers of daily newspapers, weekly journals and monthly magazines who, until a few years ago, were contented with an occasional photographic reproduction and many wood-blocks and line drawings, now insist upon having every item of interest illustrated by means of the press photograph."[63] The boroughs and townships of Central Pennsylvania were, however, not New York or London. Until the mid-1920s, photographs of local interest in the *Lewisburg Chronicle* and the *Mifflinburg Telegraph* were primarily portraits. Distant places and events were occasionally pictured in copyrighted or wire service stories. Thus, for photographs of home-town news, it was often necessary to look to postcards.

Real photo postcards were, therefore, a culmination of the visual documentation of towns in the early twentieth century. Like the illustrated books and stereographs that preceded them, postcards manifested the belief that the character of a community could be summed up by its architectural and natural features, its institutions and citizens.[64] The emphasis in these views was usually on recording and communicating facts, manifested in straightforward camera angles, lighting conditions, and printing techniques. Only rarely did the makers of real photo postcards turn from the documentary to the artistic, and then only within the prescribed boundaries of popularized versions of "camera art."

"The country is very beautiful"

When the term "art" is mentioned in discussions of pictorial postcards, it generally refers to designs by prominent graphic artists, such as Charles Dana Gibson, of "Gibson Girl" fame, or Alphonse Mucha, known for his art nouveau posters. Yet the postcard was also a medium for pictorialism, the term used to designate turn-of-the-century art photography. Pictorial photography emerged within the ranks of skilled amateurs in Europe and the United States, who sought to distinguish their work from that of commercial photographers and amateur snapshooters alike. Above all, through their associations, exhibitions, and publications, they endeavored to establish photography as a fine art.

In the United States, pictorialism was exemplified by the New York-based Photo Secession, founded in 1902; its "Little" or "291" gallery (1905-1917), which was devoted to "art" as well as to photography; the lavishly produced periodical *Camera Work* (1903-1917); and the work of its members, such as Gertrude Kasebier, Alfred Stieglitz, Edouard Steichen, and Clarence White. Pictorialism was, however, a nationwide tendency. By means of local and regional camera clubs as well as their exhibitions and publications, its aesthetic influenced photographers throughout the country.[65]

VES
PERIENCES
RG STAR CLUB

we were living in 6 feet of
at this time in tents with sheep
sleeping bags and 6 blankets to
us warm) when suddenly 15 or
Bolshevicks came out of the
ls and threatened me with hand
ades and pistols, we were stripp-
all our sidearms and hustled in-
woods, where there were about
other Bolshevicks who had got-
there without the company know-
of it, they had already dug in
machine guns so as to fire on

through the different villi,
soldiers and peasants spit at
ruck at us with whips and c
even tried to cut at us with
es. We finally arrived at H
arters which was a dirty f
tle log house, while we were t
other fellow from my same
ny and three Britishers. We
en a going over, and then pu

HOME COMING
CELEBRATION A
BIG SUCCESS

PARADE WAS LARGE AND ONE OF THE BEST SEEN IN COUNTY FOR YEARS, OTHER FEATURES GOOD.

The Union County Home Coming
Celebration held in honor if those
from the county who served our
country during the world war was
a grand success. Lewisburg was gaily
decorated and it is estimated that between five and six thousand people
were in the town.

worth while
half hour to
ut 300 soldiers
s and Y. M. C.
ine. The Red
county were
ds, the P. O. S.
from different
automobiles
pretty floats
ne of paraders.

FIRE DEST
NEAR M

STORN ON TH
OF LAST W
DAMAGE. B
LARGE QUA

The barn on
Miller, near th
Mifflinburg was
Thursday evenin
completely dest

A few minute
the structure, f
roof and befor
done the entire

There were
the barn at t
chickens and
A few loads of
destroyed.

A little girl,
Mrs. Weiser, w
was standing a
the barn and sa
She turned to
"Oh! Mamma
fell on our b

It was in the area of landscapes that art photography had the greatest impact on postcards. This is not surprising, given the artistic tastes of the American middle class, exemplified by the long-lived popularity of the nineteenth-century Hudson River and Barbizon schools of landscape painting.[66] According to M. D. S. Hymers, in *Camera and Darkroom* (1903), the countryside was the most fruitful subject for photographers in terms of "the purely artistic in pictorial art."[67] Tennant, editor of *Photo-Miniature* (1908), agreed, noting that here one could find such subjects for postcards as "a charming bit of landscape or woodland and water" that gave scope to the "individuality or personality" of the photographer, the touchstone for art photography.[68]

Pictorial photographers shunned wild mountains and manicured gardens in favor of the picturesque countryside with its meadows and woods, ponds and streams, overreaching trees, meandering paths, split rail fences, and grazing cows. These are the types of landscape subjects that were reproduced in *American Annual of Photography* and other journals which promoted the theory and practice of "artistic photography." They were also featured prominently in books such as Wallace Nutting's *Beautiful Pennsylvania* (1924), in which photographs were selected on the basis of their "pictorial interest."[69]

Such scenes also abounded in Union County, where Buffalo Creek, the Susquehanna River, McClure's "Meadow," "The Willows," and Arbutus Lane along the River Road became prime picture-taking spots for artistically inclined amateurs and professionals alike. The result was photographic images of the tracery of tree branches silhouetted against the sky, or of the play of shadows and reflections on the surface of tranquil water that merited poetic titles such as "Twilight Buffalo Creek" and "Dreamy Susquehanna."

Among local photographers, Edwin S. Heiser of Lewisburg made a particular specialty of such pictorial effects. The physical presentation of his real photo postcards was itself artful. He printed his negatives on high quality paper that he sensitized himself, used an oval mask to create a generous border around the photograph, and elegantly embossed his signature beneath the image. All of this gave his work the look of a tastefully matted studio photograph, or even of a framed drawing or lithograph, rather than that of "a mere postcard."

Moreover, Heiser's photographs were composed in such a way as to emphasize pictorial rather than reportorial values. Although less descriptive than ones made from a front and center position, angled views of streams or paths, and asymmetrical arrangements of trees or hills predominated, resulting in dynamic balances of shapes. Similarly, by rendering

riverbanks, woods, or meadows in terms of broad masses of dark and light, specific details were avoided in favor of general effects. In this way, Heiser, like other photographers of the period, sought to convey an intangible mood rather than to impart concrete information.

Although postcards by Heiser and others could be appreciated as "art for art's sake," they were also of local significance to Central Pennsylvanians. They helped foster an aesthetic appreciation of nature as well as of pictures. When a correspondent stated on a postcard of Buffalo Creek that "this is one of the many 'beauties' around Lewisburg,"[70] the reference was as much to the picturesque spot as it was to the pictorial photograph. Real photo postcards contributed to the popularization of scenic destinations for strolls, picnics, and other leisure outings. "We take our suppers at a place called 'The Willows' along the creek [in Mifflinburg], it is beautiful," commented one writer.[71] Moreover, in a region in which pastoral

---

Two views of the 1919 World War I Homecoming Parade in Lewisburg, by Nelson A. Caulkins; and a newspaper account of that event on the front page of the *Mifflinburg Telegraph*, July 18, 1919. Postcards from the collection of Gary W. and Donna M. Slear.

"Country Curves," "Overarched," "The Back Wall," and "The Renewing Year," from Wallace Nutting, *Pennsylvania Beautiful*, 1924, are typical of artistic landscape photographs of the period. From the collection of the Ellen Clarke Bertrand Library, Bucknell University.

Arbutus Lane

"The Meadows" (the side yard of the McClure home) and Arbutus Lane (south on the River Road) were among two of the Lewisburg sites that Edwin S. Heiser, with his eye for scenic beauty and artful composition, photographed sometime before 1907. From the collections of Joan Sample, and the Union County Historical Society #92.9.91.74.

charm is still considered a major asset, there was no more glowing advertisement than a real photo postcard sent from Union County with the message that "the country is very beautiful."[72]

Private Mailing Cards

Real photo postcards were, after all, "corresponding photographs." It was this unique function, which distinguished postcards from other types of photographs, that constituted their initial appeal and guaranteed their longevity. Indeed, as has been well documented by historians, the immediate impetus to the real photo postcard was provided by late-nineteenth-century innovations in postal regulations, as well as by the technical, artistic and social factors taken into account by photo historians.

In 1873, following the lead of European countries, the United States Post Office Department began issuing "correspondence cards" that could be mailed at a reduced rate. Like official postcards today, these 3¼" x 5½" cards were plain with the exception of preprinted stamps. In 1898 Congress authorized the use of privately produced cards, including pictorial cards, which could be mailed at the same rate as government-issued cards. Previously, special charters had been granted to publish private pictorial cards, for example, on the occasion of the World Columbian Exposition of 1893. However, it was this "Private Mailing Card authorized by Act of Congress of May 19, 1898" (a designation required on these cards until 1901) that facilitated the widespread production and use of real photo and other pictorial postcards.[73]

Statistics published at the time and repeated by historians provide an indication of the scope of postcard production and consumption in the United States. By 1903, half a decade after the introduction of private mailing cards, over seven and one-half million postcards were being mailed in the United States. In 1906, it was calculated that these penny postcards, including real photo postcards as well as other pictorial and plain postcards, were responsible for a 35% increase in the volume of mail throughout the country.[74]

This success was, however, dependent upon reliable and inexpensive postal service. In small towns and farming communities throughout the nation, this was achieved simultaneously with the introduction of private mailing cards by the establishment of Rural Free Delivery in 1898. Like "correspondence cards" themselves, RFD, which was subsidized by taxpayer dollars, was both praised and criticized for its democratizing function. To some, delivering mail to "ignorant" country folk with "little use" for personal letters or printed materials was a waste of money. RFD was viewed as a good investment by others, who believed it would promote the integration of rural and urban communities.[75]

At this time, post offices were housed in crossroads stores as well as in government buildings. Delivery in larger towns and in the countryside was by foot, bicycle, or horse-drawn wagon. Mail was sent to and received from across the country by train, in special carriages equipped with devices for dropping incoming mail bags on the platform and for catching outgoing mail bags suspended from posts. Remarkably, compared to today's postal vans and air mail, this "archaic" system assured same-day or overnight delivery within Union County. Indeed, at a time when the general store often possessed the only telephone in the community, postcards were one of the most expedient forms of communication available.[76]

Given its economical and efficient nature, the postcard was embraced by business. This development was anticipated by the United States Post Office Department, which announced at the time of the introduction of postcards in 1873 that they might be used for orders, price lists, and other requirements of commerce.[77] Merchants, such as J. Kleckner of C. Dreisbach's Sons Hardware in Lewisburg and F. E. Barber of Barber's Store in White Deer, used postcards to request catalogues, order merchandise, quote prices, and schedule calls.[78]

Because these postcards often featured photographs or photolithographs of the businesses themselves, they also functioned as visual advertisements.[79] Not surprisingly, individuals in the photography business were among those who employed postcards in this way. Lindig's Art Store in Lewisburg advertised products on the backs of postcards. It notified potential customers that it would be displaying not only the "Best in Post Cards and Albums" but also "novelties of every description" on the occasion of the September 1908 Lewisburg Fair. Photographer Urs H. Eisenhauer used them to arrange portrait sittings. In a card sent to a Selinsgrove, Pennsylvania, school master, he announced, "I am coming to take your school photo. Arrive the 3 or 4 Feb. 1909. You tell your pupils."[80] Like other developments in communications technology, such as the typewriter and the fax machine, the postcard was at first deemed by many to be appropriate only for business.

"Received your postal"

Nevertheless, the photo postcard became a popular vehicle — albeit a physically limited one — for personal correspondence. At the time of its inception in 1898, the plain back of the "private mailing card" was reserved for the address only. The message (when not

John Van Buskirk, mail carrier in the Winfield RD1 area, sent this postcard of himself and his postal wagon to the Boyer family on December 23, 1912. This card bore the handwritten message "Merry Christmas" and the stamp "J. A. Van Buskirk." From the collection of Ronald Nornhold. •

William "Pappy" McColm, a Civil War veteran and postal employee in the early 1900s, was photographed by Edwin S. Heiser at the railroad siding at Weikert in 1907 or later. He has positioned the mail bag so that it will be picked up by a moving train. From the collection of the Union County Historical Society #92.9.89.4. •

The messages on these postcards of the Bucknell University campus, Lewisburg, sent by a student at the beginning of the fall semester 1906, and the sanctuary of the Congregational Christian Church, North Third Street, Lewisburg (razed in 1962), sent by a parishioner at Easter 1909•, indicate the importance of educational and religious institutions and their seasonal calendars of events to the residents of Union County. From the collection of Gary W. and Donna M. Slear.

actually scrawled across the picture) was relegated to the border around the picture on the front side of the card. Beginning in 1907, however, the back was divided into a message side and an address side. This permitted writing at least on the left-hand side of the back of the card.

These physical restrictions inspired some individuals to explore novel modes of communication, such as the serialized postcard letter, consisting of a series of cards with a continuous message. On the first card in one of these series, a writer explained, "Pearl this is a combination of post-cards and letters together as it hurts my eyes to [sic] much to write a letter."[81] These postcards, which were often numbered, could be posted individually or sent together in an envelope.[82] They could be read one by one as they were received through the mail, or as a group in one sitting. The cumulative effect was described as follows by a Bucknell student, who sent four views with running commentary on the backs to a friend, "By the time

you look at all these you will have a pretty fair idea of what Lewisburg and Bucknell looks [sic] like."[83]

Most correspondents, however, seemed to regard "corresponding photographs" as a supplement to, rather than a replacement for, letters. In the messages they wrote on postcards, Central Pennsylvanians acknowledged the receipt of (or solicited) letters as well as of "postals" from their correspondents. "[Auntie] rec'd your nice letter — also the [portrait] card — this a.m. She enjoyed looking at you again, it is a fine card,"[84] was a typical response. Writers also promised letters to amplify upon the events, issues, thoughts, and sentiments expressed in the few lines that would fit on a postcard. As one writer put it, "I will explain later — when I get through with my baseball season. You know this is my busy time."[85]

Appropriately, therefore, the messages on postcards were most often devoted to brief and timely matters. In a period when travel was becoming more common, postcards were used to announce departures and arrivals. A Mifflinburg man informed friends in 1910, "Arrived home safe at 4:06 p.m. A little tired and dirty. It seems so quiet here I can scarcely stand it."[86] In a region in which friends and relatives often lived in nearby communities, postcards were a means of issuing and responding to social invitations. The following invitation was received by a Millmont

family in 1914: "We intend to have our Chx. [Christmas] entertainment on the eve of the 24th. Try & come. We want you all to see old Santa."[87] Indeed, a postcard of a train station or a hotel was adequate to assure anxious loved ones that a trip had been safely completed. Similarly, a real photo of one's home with a note such as "The latch string hangs out" and "You will not miss the place" not only extended an offer of hospitality but also provided visual directions.[88]

In a reflection of the increasing commercialization of holidays and other observances, postcards as well as greeting cards were used to send birthday, Christmas, thank you, get well, and other special greetings. As a Union County man explained in 1912,

"I will send you a picture it is to ans[wer] the purpose of a birthday card wish you a bright and happy Birthday."[89] Above all else, however, the mere act of sending a "corresponding photograph" (or a group of postcards enclosed in a letter) to a neighboring town or out of state was a way of maintaining family ties and personal friendships.

Frequently, the photograph on the front of the postcard and the message on the back were totally independent. Occasionally, however, they were mutually reinforcing, resulting in a symbiotic relationship between images and words. This calls attention to the extent to which photographs, far from speaking for themselves, gain meaning by being embedded in a discourse.[90]

L. Hartman's account of haymaking in the field north of his New Columbia farmhouse, photographed in 1908•, and Sara Bierly's description of the flowers and vines on the front porch of her Mifflinburg home, photographed by her son, "Grover," in 1915 suggest the contrasting experiences of women and men, town and country dwellers in rural Pennsylvania. From the collections of Gary W. and Donna M. Slear and the Union County Historical Society #92.9.89.58.

In September 1906, a Bucknell freshman sent a campus view with the following message to a former teacher(?) near Philadelphia: "Reached here Wed. P.M. An ideal place for college life. The annual Fresh.-Soph. contest was waged today & I came through with just a few contusions. Will write you at length when I get settled."[91] A Lewisburg woman wrote her sister in Wyoming County, New York, in April 1912, "This picture will show you how our dear little church looked on Easter. We have just put in electric lights and when our new carpet is in place we shall have as pretty an audience room as one often sees."[92]

In 1915, Sara Bierly of Mifflinburg sent a postcard of her new house to a friend. "[My son] Grover took this late in Sep, 1 year after we moved here; there was not a flower or vine when we moved here. . . . The Red geraniums cant [sic] be seen, they were lovely, only the pink and white."[93] L. Hartman of New Columbia informed his brother in July 1908, "I will send you a photo of the crew of hay makers. Just as we finished the field, north of the house, along the woods. We have a few loads of hay to make yet but might have maid [sic] it this week but I want to cut some for timothy seed I want it ripe."[94]

Contributors to general interest periodicals, including *American Illustrated Magazine*, *Atlantic*, and *Putnam's*, however, lamented the advent of corresponding photographs and not simply because of the grammatical errors evident in these examples. They were convinced that postcards, whose messages could be read by the mailman, the landlady, or the chaperon, violated privacy. Such critics were equally certain that "postals," with their meager room for writing, encouraged intellectual laziness, stifled emotional expression, and undermined literary style. It was apparently small consolation that, at a time when Hallmark and other companies were introducing greeting cards with preprinted verses, the senders of postcards were at least putting pen to paper.[95]

In "Upon the Threatened Extinction of the Art of Letter Writing" (1910), George Fitch remarked that "like a heaven-sent relief, the souvenir postal card has come to the man of few ideas and a torpid vocabulary."[96] Katharine Perry, the author of "Tirade à la carte" (1907), asked, rhetorically, whether Elizabeth and Robert Browning "Would have written those letters, passionate, prolonged/Laden with love, glittering with Greek" if they had lived in the age of the postcard.[97]

Frowned upon in "polite circles" at a time of social transformation in industrialized countries, the postcard fad was associated with "those others" as defined by economic class or by ethnic origin. Its introduction in the United States was traced to the

influx of "foreign" immigrants in the years before World War I. Similarly, its popularity in the United States and in Europe was attributed to the lack of opportunities for travel among the urban "masses" and rural "folk."[98] In this climate, the postcard was viewed as symptomatic of a general social leveling in the country and the resultant demise of "cultivated" artistic taste and "refined" social graces.

The real photo postcard was also deemed to be indicative of changes attendant to modernization, such as the hurried pace of life, which precluded leisurely letter writing, and the proliferation of photographs in newspapers and magazines, which gave these images an increasing role in communication. In "Pernicious Picture Post Card" (1906), a writer mourned the demise of "juicy letters" as follows, "Before this futile complexity of life which we call Progress had got hold upon us ...a journey was an epoch and a letter an experience."[99]

Yet, many welcomed the freedom postcards provided from the inhibiting formalities of nineteenth-century society as manifested in the prescribed etiquette of letter writing. Likewise, these individuals reveled in the increasingly rapid pace and visual character of modern experience. This was the view of Frederic T. Corkett, a representative of the British postcard publishing firm of Raphael Tuck, who addressed the Royal Society of Arts in 1906. According to Corkett, "The great utility of the picture postcard is that it enables one to do something friendly, gracefully, quickly. . . . Just 'Love from Jack,' or 'Fine place this,' and the picture does the rest. . . . It is part and parcel of the busy, rushing, time-saving age we live in."[100]

"Here's another one for your collection"

Due to its uniform size, the postcard was ideal for collecting by individuals with the leisure time and discretionary income to engage in such pursuits. Like the related pastimes of acquiring and classifying postage stamps or lithographic "scraps," postcard collecting became a popular hobby in the early years of the century. Although it had not yet been given the name deltiology (from the Greek for a small writing tablet), postcard collecting was well on its way to being formalized by means of clubs, newsletters, and exchanges.

Postcard publishers aided and abetted this hobby by offering free introductory samples, selling cards in numbered sets, organizing post card exchanges, and sponsoring collecting contests. Family Store Paper, a New York City company that advertised in the *Lewisburg Chronicle* (1911), for example, offered, "We will send you 12 of the prettiest post cards you ever saw if you will say that you will show them to your

friends. If you wish, we will also put your name on our Post Card Exchange free. You will get cards from all over the world."[101]

Postcard collecting combined the acquisitive challenge of the "carte de visite" with the educational experience of the stereo view card. Like the portrait album and the parlor stereoscope, the postcard collection was also a center of social activity in American homes. Selected cards, prized for their visual beauty, historical significance, or sentimental associations, were proudly displayed in special frames on side tables and mantelpieces. Entire collections were preserved in albums ranging from small leather-covered folios to large lacquer-bound volumes.

Predictably, Kodak marketed its own album, which was the subject of the following "testimonial" in

Kodakery (1913): "We make and send away a good many post-cards, and we wanted a special book to preserve those of our own in. We found just the thing in the [Kodak] Universal Album. The leaves in this album are made on a new principle, which does away with mounting. The prints or post-cards are merely slipped into pocket strips at top and bottom, and there you are."[102]

The postcards arranged in albums such as these included cards actually received through the mail. Indeed, for serious collectors, a postmark (sometimes obtained by mailing a card to oneself) was considered essential. Nevertheless, judging by the numbers of surviving examples with no messages or stamps, many postcards were also acquired as keepsakes. These collections were perused with interest by family

ABOVE As collected today, by locality or by subject, postcards have been decontextualized. Originally, they were part of collections, arranged in specially designed albums. Typically, collections included cards from one's own travels and those of one's friends and relatives, as well as cards with scenes and events from one's own community and those of one's correspondents. From Special Collections, Ellen Clarke Bertrand Library, Bucknell University.

RIGHT According to *American Illustrated Magazine,* whose March 1906 article on "Postal Carditis and Some Allied Manias" was accompanied by this drawing of framed postcards and a postcard album displayed on a parlor table, "Dealers have abetted this form of insanity by inventing new and diabolical designs of postal cards, as well as albums, racks and other means of preserving them. . . . Manufacturers have recently offered for sale frames, the exact size of a postal, in which some gem valued by gentle lunatics may be displayed on the walls of dens or parlors."

PAGE 42 Central Pennsylvanians could buy cameras, equipment, and supplies for making postcards at photography studios such as The Swanger Studio, Milton, which advertised in the *Lewisburg Chronicle*, October 23, 1909. Studio photographers and other professionals also provided processing services for local amateurs, who could request that their photographs be printed on postcard stock.

members and friends. Undoubtedly, to quote a critic in *Putnam's* (1907), they were also "pitilessly inflicted on the squirming casual caller."[103]

Like "cartes de visite" and other small portrait photos, which were regularly exchanged with one's intimates, postcards were manifestations of personal relationships. "The greatest pleasure we get in life is making those about us happy. Probably, that is why we always think of sending post-cards to those at

home," stated a Kodak ad in *Photo-Miniature* (1914).[104] This sentiment was echoed by a writer for *Ladies Home Journal* (1913), "Post cards indicate the thoughtfulness of our friends, and the more friends we have, the richer we are in the accumulation of these souvenirs."[105]

As was the case with stereographs of far-off places, postcards made available a vicarious form of travel and hence of education. An article in *Living Age* (1904) put it as follows, "The collector of picture-cards, if the hobby be carried out with the intelligence which it deserves, is constantly, in the imagination, traversing the whole world."[106] This belief in the educational value of postcards even prompted their being donated to local charities and overseas missions.[107]

Postcard collecting gave rise to related recreational activities. *Woman's Home Companion* published instructions for constructing a "boy's post-card projector" that could be made at home using readily available materials such a dry-goods box, a reading glass, and

a bicycle lamp, so that images and commentary could be shared with a group.[108] This magazine also outlined "parlor games," reportedly invented by a "clever high school girl," which involved identifying local, national, or international landmarks depicted on postcards.[109]

By the eve of World War I, postcard collecting (what contemporary observers with their predilection for biological metaphors called "cartomania" or "carditis") had been underway for over a decade. According to commentators on popular culture, some Americans actually found themselves in the predicament of having accumulated too many postcards. In response, the *Ladies' Home Journal*, with admirable ingenuity, suggested that its readers cut up their excess postcards and use them to create mosaic-like patterns on objects such as tabletops and screens.[110]

Postscript

Now, three-quarters of a century later, historians are putting those pieces back together. What distinguished postcards from other photographs was a format, rather than a process or a subject or a style. The real photo postcard was, however, a manifestation of the period's technical, documentary, and artistic developments, such as the growth of commercial, news, snapshot, and artistic photography. The craze relied on business' ability to create a desire for new consumer products by means of marketing. These included postcards themselves, as well as equipment and supplies for studio and lay photographers, and accessories such as albums for collectors.

The diversity of amateur and professional producers, in a field in which almost anyone could be a publisher of real photo postcards, and the availability of a range of images, from the most public to the most private, are evidence of photography's role in the democratization of images. By giving rural America the ability to picture itself in portraits and views, the postcard corroborated the role of photography in constructing individual and community identities.

A relatively rapid form of communication, in which pictures were expected to do at least some of the talking, the postcard introduced "you press the button, we do the rest" and "a picture is worth a thousand words" approaches to correspondence. As such, the real photo postcard, which exemplified the instantaneousness and reproducibility of the photographic medium, was an integral part of the increasingly accelerated pace and visual character of early twentieth-century American culture.

[1] Then, as now, articles on postcards published in art journals were devoted to reproductions of "old masters" or original works by "fine artists." See Mary Beard, "Souvenirs of Culture: Deciphering (in) the Museum," *Art History* 15 (December 1992): 505-32; Dominique Lerch, "La carte postale, son histoire, sa fonction sociale," *Gazette des beaux-arts* 107 (March 1986): 131-32; Laurence Pythoud, "La carte postale," *L'Oeil* no. 447 (December 1992): 68-71.

[2] Frank L. Emanuel, "Pictorial Postcards: A General Survey," *Magazine of Art* 27 (December 1902): 87.

[3] Katharine Perry, "Tirade à la carte," *Putnam's Magazine* 3 (December 1907): 336.

[4] See Dorothy S. Gelatt, "Antique Postcards on the Move — 20¢ to $20,000," *Maine Antique Digest* (January 1995): 12-D, 13-D; Robert Ward, *Investment Guide to North American Real Photo Postcards,* 2nd ed. (Bellevue, Wa.: Antique Paper Guild, 1993), iii.

[5] See, for example, assessment by Kim Keister, "Wish You Were Here: The Curt Teich Postcard Archives," *Historic Preservation* 44 (March-April 1992): 54, 58-59.

[6] My discussion is indebted to these general studies, as well as to the specific studies and primary sources indicated in subsequent notes: Richard Carline, *Pictures in the Post: The Story of the Picture Postcard and Its Place in the History of Popular Art,* 2nd ed. (Philadelphia: Deltiologists of America, 1972); Hal Morgan and Andreas Brown, *Prairie Fires and Paper Moons: The American Photographic Postcard, 1900-1920* (Boston: David R. Godine, 1981); Martin Parr and Jack Stasiak, *'The Actual Boot': The Photographic Post Card Boom, 1900-1920* (Bradford, West Yorkshire, England: The National Museum of Photography Film and Television, 1986); Dorothy B. Ryan, *Picture Postcards in the United States, 1893-1918,* rev. ed. (New York: C. N. Potter, 1982); Frank Staff, *The Picture Postcard and Its Origins,* 2nd ed. (London: Lutterworth Press, 1979).

[7] Although numerous other publications could be cited here, these examples indicate the range of current studies. See: George Miller, *A Pennsylvania Album: Picture Postcards, 1900-1930* (University Park: Pennsylvania State University Press, 1979); R. Brewster Harding, *Roadside New England 1900-1955* (Portland, Me.: Old Port Publishing Co., 1982); Keister, "Wish You Were Here," 4-61; John Baeder, *Gas, Food, and Lodging* (New York: Abbeville Press, 1982).

[8] See William C. Darrah, *Cartes de Visite in Nineteenth-Century Photography* (Gettysburg, Pa.: Times and News Publishing Co., 1981); Elizabeth Anne McCauley, *A. A. E. Disdéri and the Carte de Visite Portrait Photograph* (New Haven: Yale University Press, 1985); William C. Darrah, *Stereo Views: A History of Stereographs in America and Their Collection* (Gettysburg, Pa.: Times and News Publishing Co., 1964); Edward Earle, ed., *Points of View: The Stereograph in America — A Cultural History* (Rochester: The Visual Studies Workshop, 1979).

[9] See Jonathan Green, *American Photography: A Critical History 1945 to the Present* (New York: Harry N. Abrams, 1984).

[10] See Walker Evans, "Main Street Looking North from Courthouse Square," *Fortune* (May 1948): 102-06; Jonathan Green, ed., *The Snap-Shot* (Millerton, N.Y.: Aperture, 1974).

[11] See advertising circular for the Lindig Art Studio, c. 1908, John Van Buskirk collection, Lewisburg, Pa.

[12] For the prices of staple grocery items, see advertisements for Mifflinburg Markets, J. D. S. Gast & Son's, and Eureka Bakery in the *Mifflinburg (Pa.) Telegraph*, April 3, 1908, April 24, 1908, and May 15, 1908. In 1909, monthly wages at The Glen Iron Furnace, Pa., were between $25 and $40. See Time Book, Glen Iron Furnace/John Thomas Church, June 1, 1902-August 31, 1913, Union County Historical Society, Lewisburg, Pa..

[13] D. Campbell, "Picture Postcards," *American Amateur Photographer* 18 (August 1906): 393.

[14] "The Amateur as Business Spoiler," *Abel's Photographic Weekly,* 4 (August 28, 1909): 1.

[15] See John W. Ripley, "The Art of Postcard Fakery," *The Kansas Historical Quarterly* 38 (summer 1972): 129-31.

[16] For a case study of a publishing industry leader, see Keister, "Wish You Were Here," 54-61.

[17] "Fancy Goods and Notions," *Dry Goods Economist* (1905), quoted in Ryan, *Picture Postcards,* 16.

[18] *Photographic Journal of America* 52 (December 1915): 15. See also advertisement for Gatchel & Manning, Philadelphia, in *Abel's Photographic Weekly* 3 (December 12, 1908): 23.

[19] See "The Place of Portrait Postcards in a Professional Business," *Abel's Photographic Weekly* 3 (February 6, 1909): 106-07.

[20] *Mifflinburg (Pa.) Telegraph*, November 1, 1907.

[21] "A Small-Town Photographer," *Abel's Photographic Weekly* 4 (Oct 2, 1909): 92-93; "Some Hints on Business Novelties," *Abel's Photographic Weekly* 3 (February 27, 1909): 143.

[22] For the history of these fields, see David E. Nye, "Early American Commercial Photography: Origins, Techniques and Esthetics," *Journal of American Culture* 6 (fall 1983): 1-13; Robert E. Snyder and Jack B. Moore, *Pioneer Commercial Photography: The Burgert Brothers, Tampa, Florida* (Gainesville: University Press of Florida, 1992); Marianne Fulton, *Eyes of Time: Photojournalism in America* (Boston: New York Graphic Society, 1988).

[23] "A Small-Town Photographer," 92. Consequently, journals such as *Photo-Miniature* published articles on various aspects of commercial practice. See "Commercial Photography," *Photo-Miniature* 4 (March 1903): 561-600; C. H. Claudy, "Press Photography," *Photo-Miniature* 5 (June 1903): 97-134; Henry C. Delery, "Architectural Photography," *Photo-Miniature* 5 (October 1903): 289-333.

[24] That there was a need for additional views in some parts of the county was observed by a correspondent who, on a postcard sent

from Millmont, Pa., to Lewisburg, Pa., in 1907, stated, "I am sorry the views up here are not very nice." This card is #94.7.2, Union County Historical Society collection.

25 John A. Tennant, ed., "Photographic Post-Cards," *Photo-Miniature* 8 (October 1908): 424.

26 M. E. S. Hymers, "Amateur Photography that Pays," *Camera and Darkroom* 6 (May 1903): 151-54.

27 This type of real photo postcard is little valued by collectors and rarely discussed by historians. See Ward, *Investment Guide*, iii, vi., viii.

28 See Brian Coe and Paul Gates, *The Snapshot Photograph: The Rise of Popular Photography 1888-1939* (London: Ash & Grant, 1977).

29 Charles E. Fairman, "Photographic Post-Cards," *Camera and Darkroom* 7 (January 1904): 9-14; Percy L. Slater, "Printing and Developing the Picture Postcard," *Camera and Darkroom* 8 (June 1905): 178-80; Campbell, "Picture Postcards," 393; Tennant, "Photographic Post-Cards," 423-59; E. J. Wall and H. Snowden Ward, *The Photographic Picture Post-Card* (London: Dawbarn and Ward, 1906). Unless indicated otherwise, all technical information, an aspect that has received little attention in recent studies of postcards, is from these period sources.

30 See two postcards in the Gary W. and Donna M. Slear collection, Lewisburg, Pa. These were sent by Sara Bierly of Mifflinburg, Pa. (apparently in an envelope as there is no address, stamp, or postmark) to a friend in 1915. Although these real photo postcards of the Bierly home were printed by Sara Bierly, they were taken by her son William "Grover" Bierly. On the first she noted, "I had to 'squint' as we stood in the sun. I printed it a little too dark." On the second she remarked, "Kitty & I got on the picture, but just as Grover 'snapped' the kitty moved."

31 "This picture is not clear but you can imagine what it was like." Postcard of Bucknell class rush, sent to South Amboy, N.J., October 9, 1906, Slear collection. "Nell, here we are. First picture not good, same not properly focused." Postcard of Lewisburg train station, sent to Millersburg, Pa., January 9, 1908, Slear collection.

32 "What causes the brown up in the left hand corner? I think it wasn't hypoed enough. This is the only one that has been no good so far. One or two have the upper corner brown just over the pennant hanging over the picture but everything else is clear. Is not the white streak over the window & cosy corner caused by improper development of the film? I used new developer on these but old hypo." Postcard of Bucknell fraternity house interior sent from Lewisburg, Pa., to Pittsburgh, Pa., February 17, 1909, Slear collection. See inside cover for a reproduction of this card.

33 "I thought you might like this picture of our dining room. It is a flashlight William took the evening before the reception." Postcard sent (apparently in an envelope as there is no address, stamp or postmark) to Muncy, Pa., 1907 or later, Jeannette Lasansky collection, Lewisburg, Pa.

34 Primary and secondary sources are in disagreement concerning the "standard" dimensions of real photo postcards. Although the dimensions 3½" x 5½" appear in the literature, 3¼" x 5½" will be used here. The dimensions 3¼" x 5½" are specified in some instructional articles. See Fairman, "Photographic Post-Cards," 10. Kodak's "postcard" cameras, including the Folding Pocket Kodak No. 3A, made 3¼" x 5½" negatives. See Coe and Gates, *The Snapshot Photograph*, 25, 31-33. The dimensions 3¼" x 3½" are also stipulated in local postal guides. See *The Complete Directory and Post Office Guide: Lewisburg, West Lewisburg, and Four Rural Routes* (Lewisburg, Pa.: W. E. Housel, postmaster, 1911), 98.

35 See James M. McKeown and Joan C. McKeown, eds., *Price Guide to Antique and Classic Still Cameras*, 4th ed. (Grantsburg, Wisc.: Centennial Photo Service, 1983); Coe and Gates, *The Snapshot Photograph*, 25, 31-33.

36 See William Crawford, *The Keepers of Light: A History and Working Guide to Early Photographic Processes* (Dobbs Ferry, N.Y.: Morgan & Morgan, 1979).

37 See Naomi Rosenblum, "Short Technical History" sections in *A World History of Photography* (New York: Abbeville Press, 1989).

38 See Douglas Collins, *The Story of Kodak* (New York: Harry N. Abrams, 1990).

39 "Colored Vacation Post-Cards," *Photo-Miniature* 12 (July 1914): n. p.

40 In addition to advertisements reproduced here, see "Kodak Amateur Printer," *Camera* 7 (August 1915): 141; "Kodak Film Tank," *Kodakery* (September 1913): n.p.; "Argo Post Cards," *American Photography* 5 (July 1907): n.p.

41 Contrary to popular belief, it was not necessary to use an Autographic Kodak, which permitted writing on the film while it was still in the camera, in order to apply titles to real photo post-cards. For the Autographic Kodak, which was introduced in 1914 and was available in a 3A "postcard" model, see "The Autographic Kodak," *Kodakery* 2 (September 1914): 10-14; Coe and Gates, *The Snapshot Photograph*, 31-33.

42 See "Aerial Photography," *Photo-Miniature* 5 (July 1903): 145-73; "Street Photography," *Photo-Miniature* 2 (May 1900): 1-88.

43 Wall and Ward, *The Photographic Picture Post-Card*, 75.

44 Tennant, "Photographic Post-Cards," 425.

45 Campbell, "Picture Postcards," 393.

46 Tennant, "Photographic Post-Cards," 425. See also Wall and Ward, *The Photographic Picture Post-Card*, 75-76.

47 Tennant, "Photographic Post-Cards," 426.

48 Wall and Ward, *The Photographic Picture Post-Card*, 76.

49 See, for example, William Ide, "Winter Photography," *Camera and Darkroom* 6 (November 1903): 401-04; W. H. Broadwell, "Night Photography," *American Annual of Photography* 23 (1909): 68-71.

50 Tennant, "Photographic Post-Cards," 452.

51 Campbell, "Picture Postcards," 393. See also Hymers, "Amateur Photography that Pays," 153, who recommended making up a sample booklet of photographs of one's own home to show to prospective customers.

52 Hymers, "Amateur Photography that Pays," 151-54.

53 Tennant, "Photographic Post-Cards," 424.

54 Fairman, "Photographic Post-Cards," 14.

55 Interview with Betty Hagey Herald, Watsontown, Pa., September 26, 1995.

56 See especially Jay Ruby, "Images of Rural America," *History of Photography* 12 (October/December 1988): 327-43.

57 Eli Bowen, *Pictorial Sketchbook of Pennsylvania* (Philadelphia: W. White Smith, 1854), 9-10.

58 Earl Shinn, *A Century After: Picturesque Glimpses of Philadelphia and Pennsylvania* (Philadelphia: Allen, Lane & Scott and J. W. Lauderbach, 1875), 297-98.

59 John Walker Harrington, "Postal Carditis and Some Allied Manias," *American Illustrated Magazine* 61 (March 1906): 562-67.

60 Hymers, "Amateur Photography that Pays," 151-54.

61 Robert Jay, *The Trade Card in Nineteenth-Century America* (Columbia: University of Missouri Press, 1987). Generally, these were 3"x5" cards with lithographs advertising a brand-name product on the front and information concerning a local merchant on the back. Occasionally, however, smaller 2½" x 4" or 4½" calling card photographs of a business, its employees, or its products were used for this purpose.

[62] Raymond Smith Schuneman, "The Photograph in Print: An Examination of New York Daily Newspapers, 1890-1937," Ph.D. diss., University of Minnesota, 1966, 97-100, cited in Nye, "Early American Commercial Photography," 3.

[63] John Everard, *Photographs for the Papers: How to Take and Place Them,* 2nd ed. (London: A. and C. Black, Ltd, 1923), 9.

[64] See Cervin Robinson and Joel Herschman, *Architecture Transformed: A History of the Photography of Buildings from 1839 to the Present* (Cambridge, Mass.: The MIT Press, 1987), 64, 72; Colin Westerbeck and Joel Meyerowitz, *Bystander: A History of Street Photography* (Boston: Little, Brown and Company, 1994), 82.

[65] For standard and revisionist accounts of pictorial photography and criticism see: William Innes Homer, *Alfred Stieglitz and the Photo-Secession* (Boston: Little, Brown, 1983); Ulrich Keller, "The Myth of Art Photography," Parts I and II, *History of Photography* 8 (October/December 1984): 249-75; 9 (January/March 1985): 1-38.

[66] See Barbara Novak, *Nature and Culture: American Landscape and Painting, 1825-1875* (New York: Oxford University Press, 1980); Estelle Jussim and Elizabeth Lindquist-Cock, *Landscape as Photograph* (New Haven: Yale University Press, 1985).

[67] Hymers, "Amateur Photography that Pays," 151-54.

[68] Tennant, "Photographic Post-Cards," 425. See also Charles Stillman Taylor, "The Study and Appreciation of Nature," *American Annual of Photography* 23 (1909): 153-63.

[69] Wallace Nutting, *Pennsylvania Beautiful* (Norwood, Mass.: The Plimpton Press, 1924), 3-4.

[70] Postcard sent from Lewisburg, Pa., to Saltsburg, Pa., 1906, #92.9.91.75, Union County Historical Society collection.

[71] Undated postcard sent from Mifflinburg, Pa., to Lock Haven, Pa., #83.35.24, Union County Historical Society collection.

[72] Postcard sent from Mifflinburg, Pa., to Lancaster County, Pa., 1907 or later, Slear collection.

[73] See Frederic T. Corkett, "The Production and Collection of the Pictorial Postcard," *Journal of the Society of Arts* 54 (April 27, 1906): 622-33; histories of pictorial postcards listed above. These officially mandated changes, along with postmarks and trademarks, permit the dating of real photo postcards. See Morgan and Brown, *Prairie Fires*, 187-90.

[74] Corkett, "The Production and Collection of the Pictorial Postcard," 625; Harrington, "Photographic Post-Cards," 562-67.

[75] See George B. Cortelyou, "The Rural Delivery Service," *Independent* 61 (August 9, 1906): 303-07.

[76] See Richard A. Haste, "The Northwest Mail," *World Today* 8 (April 1905): 415-23.

[77] See Staff, *The Picture Postcard*, 86.

[78] See postcard sent from J. H. Kleckner to Port Treverton, Pa., 1908, Slear collection; postcard sent from F. E. Barber to Lewisburg, Pa., 1907 or later, Slear collection.

[79] Indeed, Union County businesses utilized postcards in this way from the time of their introduction in the 1870s. See examples of plain, official postcards, the earliest of which is dated 1878, in the Union County Historical Society collection.

[80] From the Ronald Nornhold collection, Troxelville, Pa.

[81] Unfortunately, the other cards in this series are lost. As they were mailed in an envelope, the writer, recipient, and date are unknown. This postcard is in the Slear collection.

[82] Apparently, there was some concern that postcards might be damaged if not mailed in an envelope. "I received your post card. It was not spoiled," wrote a correspondent on a postcard sent from Lewisburg, Pa., to Kingston, N.H., April 29, 1912. This postcard is #89.15.23, the Union County Historical Society collection.

[83] Four postcards sent from Lewisburg, Pa., to Oneida, N.Y., May 2, 1908, Slear collection.

[84] Postcard of Lewisburg, Pa., sent to Mullica Hill, N.J., October 21, 1908, Slear collection.

[85] Postcard sent from Lewisburg, Pa., to Pine Grove, Pa., June 23, 1909, Slear collection.

[86] Postcard sent from Mifflinburg, Pa., to Turtle Creek, Pa., July 10, 1909, #83.38.8, Union County Historical Society collection

[87] Postcard sent from Mifflinburg, Pa., to Millmont, Pa., December 17, 1914, #83.37.3, Union County Historical Society collection.

[88] Postcard sent from Lewisburg, Pa., to Port Jervis, N.Y., September 8(?), 1906, Slear collection; postcard sent from Millmont, Pa., to Washington, D.C., September 24, 1909, #90.21.10, Union County Historical Society collection.

[89] Postcard sent to Barbara Watson, 1912, Jeffrey L. Mensch collection, Mifflinburg, Pa.

[90] Allan Sekula, "On the Invention of Photographic Meaning," *Artforum* 13 (January 1975): 36-45.

[91] Postcard sent from Lewisburg, Pa., to Bustleton, Pa., September 29(?), 1906, Slear collection.

[92] Postcard sent from Lewisburg, Pa., to Castile, Wyoming County, N.Y., April 17, 1912, Slear collection.

[93] Postcard sent (apparently in an envelope because there is no address, stamp, or postmark) from Mifflinburg, Pa., 1915, Slear collection.

[94] Postcard sent (apparently in an envelope because there is no address, stamp, or postmark) from New Columbia, Pa., July 17, 1908, #92.9.89.58, Union County Historical Society collection.

[95] See Joyce Hall, *When You Care Enough* (Kansas City, Mo.: Hallmark, 1992); Ellen Stern, *The Very Best from Hallmark Greeting Cards through the Years* (New York: Harry N. Abrams, 1988).

[96] George Fitch, "Threatened Extinction of the Art of Letter Writing," *American Illustrated Magazine* 70 (June 1910): 172.

[97] Perry, "Tirade à la carte," 336.

[98] See Harrington, "Photographic Post-Cards," 562-67; and "Picture Post-Cards," *Living Age* 242 (July 30, 1904): 310-14.

[99] "Pernicious Picture Post Card," *Atlantic* 98 (August 1906): 288.

[100] Corkett, "The Production and Collection of the Pictorial Postcard," 624.

[101] *Lewisburg (Pa.) Chronicle*, June 17, 1911, p. 3.

[102] "A Pleasurable Reform," *Kodakery* 1 (October 1913): 24.

[103] Perry, "Tirade à la carte," 336.

[104] "Colored Vacation Post-Cards," n. p.

[105] S. D. Prixe, "What to Do with Your Post Cards," *Ladies Home Journal* 30 (March 1913): 98.

[106] "Picture Post-Cards," *Living Age*, 310-14.

[107] Ibid.; Prixe, "What to Do with Your Post Cards," 98.

[108] A. E. Swoyer, "A Boy's Post-Card Projector," *Woman's Home Companion* 39 (April 1912): 28.

[109] Rosalie Dawson, "Fun with Picture Postal Cards," *Woman's Home Companion* 33 (February 1906): 56.

[110] Prixe, "What to Do with Your Post Cards," 98. See also Harrington, "Photographic Post-Cards," 562-67.

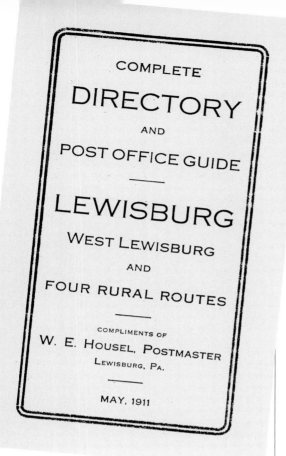

COMPLETE
DIRECTORY
AND
POST OFFICE GUIDE

LEWISBURG
WEST LEWISBURG
AND
FOUR RURAL ROUTES

COMPLIMENTS OF
W. E. HOUSEL, POSTMASTER
LEWISBURG, PA.

MAY, 1911

The cover and three pages of the 100-page *Complete Directory* are illustrated here. From the collection of William and Jeannette Lasansky.

PREFACE

This Directory of Lewisburg, West Lewisburg, and the adjacent territory covered by four Rural Delivery Routes, together with a vast amount of postal information, presents in compact form and extraordinary completeness many things the public should know about postal affairs but have no means of learning except by inquiring of their postmaster, whose answers must frequently be hurriedly given, perhaps unsatisfactory even unto himself, and the information thus obtained is liable to be forgotten, confused or misconstrued the next time needed.

To remedy this apparent evil, by attempting to answer in concise form, the questions most frequently asked at post office windows, pointing out the errors commonly made by otherwise well informed people and suggesting how to avoid them, and giving to the public the only complete Directory ever published of Lewisburg, West Lewisburg and all surrounding territory, is the principal mission of this little booklet, and if the contents shall give to those who possess a copy, through the courtesy of their postmaster, a better understanding and higher appreciation of the postal service, and residential addresses of all those who reside in Lewisburg, West Lewisburg and along four rural routes, it will not have been prepared in vain.

This booklet is designed to be a thoroughly reliable and strictly up-to-date reference book which will be found equally useful in the school, the office and the home. In addition to the vast amount of postal information there will be found the name and address of every person in Lewisburg, West Lewisburg, Rural Routes 1, 2, 3 and Milton No. 4, from the head of a family down to those of ten and fifteen years of age, in alphabetical order, the greatest care being exercised that not a single individual be omitted.

W. E. HOUSEL.

RATES OF POSTAGE ON POST CARDS.

Post Cards of same size and material as Postal Card ....1c.

Post Cards of different size or material with writing ....2c.
Same without writing ....1c.

Leather Post Cards with writing....2c.

Leather Post Cards without writing ....1c.

Birch Bark Post Cards, with writing ....2c.

Birch Bark Post Cards, without writing ....1c.

Post Cards enclosed in thin envelopes with writing ....2c.
Same unsealed and without writing..1c.

Post Cards, with small envelopes attached, unsealed, without writing.......1c.
Same, with writing ....2c.
Same, sealed ....2c.

Post Cards with tinsel on are unmailable unless enclosed in envelopes and are sent direct to the Dead Letter Office.

Post Cards in envelopes must have the stamp attached to the envelope instead of the card; no matter if the envelope is of thin paper or has a hole in it. Put your stamps on the envelope if you want it to go.

Post Cards bearing particles of mica, glass, tinsel, sand or other similar substance are unmailable, except when enclosed in tightly sealed envelopes.

MAILS DISPATCHED.

Time of Mail.	Time of Train.	Railroad
6:00 a. m. west	6:30 a. m.	L. & T.
8:30 a. m. south	9.00 a. m.	Penna.
9:15 a. m. north	9:45 a. m.	Penna.
10:50 a. m. south	11:00 a. m.	Reading
11:13 a. m. north	11:43 a. m.	Reading
12:45 p. m. south	1:15 p. m.	Penna.
12:45 p. m. north	1:15 p. m.	Penna.
1:20 p. m. west	1:50 p. m.	L. & T.
3:56 p. m. south	4:26 p. m.	Penna.
3:56 p. m. north	4:24 p. m.	Penna.
4:25 p. m. south	4:55 p. m.	Reading
4:50 p. m. north	5:20 p. m.	Reading
5:20 p. m. west to Mfg.	5:40 p. m.	Penna.
6:17 p. m. south	6:47 p. m.	L. & T.
7:25 p. m. no'th & so'th	9:50 p. m.	Penna.
4:15 p. m. south, Sun.	4:45 p. m.	Reading Penna.

MAILS RECEIVED.

Time of Train.
6:00 a. m. from north and south via P. R. R.
6:30 a. m. from the south via Penna. R. R.
9:00 a. m. from Mifflinburg and west.
9:37 a. m. from the north via Penna. R. R.
10:13 a. m. from the south via Penna. R. R.
11:00 a. m. from the north via P. & R.
11:43 a. m. from the south via P. & R.
1:50 p. m. from north and south via P. R. R.
4:25 p. m. from Mifflinburg and west.
4:25 p. m. from the south via P. & R.
4:55 p. m. from the north via P. & R.
5:07 p. m. from the north via P. R. R.
5:55 p. m. from the south via Penna. R. R.
6:40 p. m. from Mifflinburg via L. T. R. R.
7:00 a. m. SUNDAY from north and south via Penna. R. R. by special messenger from Montandon.

All mails are closed at the office thirty minutes prior to the scheduled time of departure of train.

No mail received on Sunday except at 7:00 a. m., from all points north, east, south and west.

No mail dispatched on Sunday except at 4:15 p. m. for all points north, east, south and west.

Union County: Prosperous, Progressive and Growing

by Jeannette Lasansky

Introduction

Each generation has always remarked on the momentous changes it has witnessed. The first decades of the twentieth century were no different in this regard, but the changes would come faster and reach further than before. Generally they were viewed as positive. The changes would encompass communication, transportation, agriculture, education, and the role of government. In rural areas, like Central Pennsylvania, these changes would blend with long familiar landscapes, celebrations, and personalities. Local towns, like Lewisburg and Mifflinburg, moved from the Gilded Age into the Progressive Era.[1]

What Americans experienced in these first decades would be captured not only in their letters, diaries, day books, newspapers, and oral accounts, as in the past, but also in photographs. The photographs could be taken by oneself or a neighborly camera enthusiast. No longer confined to a studio setting or to docu-mentation of what others considered important, such as soldiers going off to war, local photographs would capture meaningful everyday events: people with their pets, families doing chores, the construction of a new bridge, or the paving of a road or sidewalk, as well as a parade or local disaster.

"Corresponding photographs," also called real photo postcards, became popular among rural Americans. Individuals could communicate with a combination of specifically chosen visual material and words by purchasing what others photographed locally and marketed at area stores or by snapping, developing, and printing their own images on postcard stock. Postcards served in place of letters on days when "eyes were weary,"[2] when one had to write "hastily,"[3] when sending birthday or seasonal greetings, as a form or reminder of business arrangements, and as a conveyor of shared sense of place. It is not surprising that these cards became "a fad"[4] soon after they

46

appeared in the first years of the twentieth century, facilitated in large part by changes in the American postal system and regulations.

These cards also combined the need to stay in touch with an interest in the collection and presentation of visual material. People began to assemble postcards as they had previously gathered scraps, autographs, and mementos. The *Mifflinburg Telegraph* of February 28, 1913, noted in its "Personals" column, "Recently, on her 80th birthday anniversary, Mrs. Mary Balliet of East Chestnut St., received a shower of over a hundred post cards, carrying good cheer to the heart of the esteemed old lady. Many were from friends in the West." Cards like Mary Balliet's — whether they consisted of corresponding photographs, photolithographic views, or greetings by Hallmark or C.A. Reed — would then be assembled in albums to be looked at from time to time.

The focus of this book is on the first four decades of the twentieth century, 1905-1935. The real photo postcards from Union County serve as a record of what rural America looked like then as well as what was important to residents. While this type of postcard was issued here until the early 1940s, the majority of the cards date from 1905 to 1920, when they were at the height of fashion. Their popularity tapered off in the 1930s. Other types of postcards — the linens of the 1930s and 1940s and the post-World War II chromes — though not as personal, became more popular. These later postcards were produced commercially and in larger numbers.

One overriding theme in the real photo postcards is a strong sense of place — both the built environment: the schools, churches, businesses, and homes — as well as the natural. Bounded on the east by the Susquehanna River, Union County's rich farmlands lie within Pennsylvania's ridge and valley system. The county is bounded by a series of ridges that arc from the southwest to the northeast, forming its western and northern perimeters. Penns Creek defines the southern edge. Waterways and varied land forms were featured prominently in period photography. These photographs were taken from afar, as in the "bird's-eye" views, or in closer detail.

The other major theme in the cards is the focus on modernity — images of newly built bridges, dams, and roads, which reinforced the area's relative prosperity and its progressive nature. The cards complement the fervor of the local newspaper editors. These postcards promoted Central Pennsylvania before there were chambers of commerce or economic development councils.

The absence of certain subjects in the postcards is curious. For instance, people were not shown with their bicycles although they were very popular,[5] and the Chautauqua was captured only once in card format even though it was a major focus of summer cultural life in Union County from 1912 to 1931.

The following 175 cards were selected from over 1,000 real photo postcards in private collections as well as in the collection of the Union County Historical Society. Photographs of buildings (devoid of people, animals, or vehicles) which still stand and which, if photographed today, would look essentially the same were not chosen for reproduction. Also limited in representation are streetscapes, many of which have few identifying features, and individual or group portraits. The picturesque setting of willows along creeks in Lewisburg and Mifflinburg, scenes which were taken repeatedly over time and from many different angles, were also restricted to a few examples. Postcards were also chosen for their clarity and depth of contrast.

The postcards are grouped by themes in this section, with accompanying text based as much as possible on contemporary newspaper accounts in the weekly *Lewisburg Chronicle* and *Mifflinburg Telegraph* or from the serialized history of Union County published by R.V.B. Lincoln from 1899 to 1902. The captions indicate if photolithographic versions were made of the real photo view. Current or earlier place names are indicated in parentheses when they differ from the early twentieth-century names. Cards are dated by using one or more of the following: the date of the subject matter, references in the correspondence section of the card, notes added later, and postmarks, as well as the style of the cards' backs. The cards' photographers or publishers are indicated when they are known. One

---

LEFT A Pennsy American-type locomotive leads a three-car train into Lewisburg on the Lewisburg & Tyrone branch. The train comes across the new steel railroad bridge as construction debris lies in the foreground, and the "free bridge" is seen on the right. This card was sent from Lewisburg on September 10, 1912, to Mrs. Mary DeValle in Trenton, New Jersey. The correspondent, Estella, wrote, "Your card rec'd, thanks. Here is a view of the Old bridge after they had two span[s] up. They expect to be done in about three week[s]. I think they have them all up but two span[s] now. It makes quite a change at our end of town." From the collection of Union County Historical Society #92.9.91.133. •

The Chautauqua tent on Loomis Field, Bucknell University, was photographed by Edwin S. Heiser in the summer c. 1922. Dr. Emory Hunt was instrumental in bringing the cultural, religious, recreational movement to Lewisburg in the 1920s and 1930s. Daytime educational seminars and evening performances were held in the tent. From the collection of Joan Sample. •

"Old Canal" at Montandon, Pa.

or more bullet(s) • at the end of a caption means only one card has been found of a particular view. Most of these postcards have not been published since they were originally issued between 1905 and 1935.

Relics and Pilgrimages

Local newspapers of the early twentieth century gave nostalgia little time or space except for their coverage of Memorial Day celebrations, family reunions, and the programs and pilgrimages of the county's new historical society or the local chapter of the DAR. Similarly, real photo postcards were limited to just a few commemorative sites or events.

One such event depicted on a postcard was the dedication of a memorial marker for Samuel Maclay near his eighteenth-century home. John R. Mench, who wrote a letter to the editor of the *Mifflinburg Telegraph* on November 30, 1906, argued the need for such commemorative events:

Few of our people in Union County know that in Buffalo Township Hon. Samuel Maclay is buried on Mr. Howard Green's farm, one of Pennsylvania's statesmen. He was a member of the United States Senate, also one of the first land surveyors of Buffalo Valley. He owned extensive real estate in Union County . . . Hon. Samuel Maclay was one of the first members of the Buffalo Crossroads Presbyterian Church. He was personally acquainted with the youngest son of the Indian Chief Shikellamy of the Six Nations.[6]

Two postcards illustrate historic limestone structures in Winfield. One is a photograph of Abraham Eyer's stone barn, the site where a conference of the Evangelical Church met June 11-13, 1816, when the church established its first "frontier" missionary outreach program (to Ohio) and its publishing house (in New Berlin). The other card is of the John Lee family's stone spring house, which was at or near the site where the last Indian massacre in the area occurred in 1782. Both cards were popular enough to be reissued in black-and-white photolithographic versions which included explanatory captions. Interest in and concern about the Lee massacre site appeared in the *Mifflinburg Telegraph* on September 11, 1930:

Several historical organizations have been asked to take over the place before time has had a chance to work havoc with the structure. It was on August 13, 1782 and with thirteen gathered around the dinner table that the Indians surprised Major John Lee and his family. Only two of the party were left, the others were either killed or carried off as captives by the Indians, later being brought to Fort Augusta, at Sunbury. Some years later three of the children who had been captured were rescued by the son of Major Lee, who was not in the house at the time of the attack. It was quite some time until they became accustomed to civilization, but finally did and settled down to a happy married life at the old Lee Homestead.

A glass plate negative of the Montandon/Lewisburg cross-cut canal (active 1833-1869) was reissued as a real photo postcard by photographer Stephen B. Horton c. 1911. Two barges are evident in the scene labeled "Old Canal." Horton also made a real photo postcard of Montandon's Main Street about the same time. From the collection of Helen Hopp.•

The Samuel Maclay homestead was photographed from its southern exposure in 1908. Maclay's eighteenth-century stone house is still standing at the end of a private lane almost directly opposite the Dreisbach Church on Dreisbach Church Road in Buffalo Township. The photograph was one of only a few local photographs to appear in the county newspapers in the 1910s. From the collection of the Union County Historical Society #92.9.89.44.

The newly erected Maclay monument was photographed with construction debris in the foreground and workers on the left. The monument, dedicated on October 16, 1908, is located in the cemetery of the Dreisbach Church. From the collection of Gary W. and Donna M. Slear. •

The stone barn, built in 1805 on Abraham Eyer's farm in Winfield, was the site of an important Evangelical Church conference in 1816. On the left is the road heading south to Shamokin Dam and Selinsgrove, while in front is the road through Winfield. The barn was demolished when Route 15 (formerly the Lewisburg/Winfield Road) was widened in the early 1960s. The real photo postcard was issued as early as 1907 and in a black-and-white photolithographic version. From the collection of Gary W. and Donna M. Slear.

LEWISBURG, PA.

Local history was being promoted here in the early 1900s by individuals like Dr. George G. Groff; Professor D. P. Stapleton, the superintendent of Union County schools; and Reverend W. H. Shloch of New Berlin. Together, these men called upon area residents to remember area historical events by writing about them in the local newspapers. In 1906, along with others, the three men organized the Union County Historical Society. The interests of the society's founders focused on eighteenth-century people, sites, and events: the Maclays, the Old Presbyterian Church at Buffalo Cross Roads (organized in 1773), and the massacres, particularly the LeRoy Massacre of 1755.

At the LeRoy Massacre site in Limestone Township, annual memorials were held on the massacre's anniversary date of October 16. In 1919 the county and state historical societies jointly erected a monument nearby to commemorate this massacre, the first in a series of locally significant events during the French and Indian War. Over 300 attended the marker's dedication.[7] A good crowd also began attending the annual spring or fall "pilgrimages and reunions" held at the Old Presbyterian Church in Buffalo Cross Roads.

Of these various sites and events, only the LeRoy Massacre site was not recorded in real photo postcards of the period.

Three other "historic" postcard subjects were actually reissues of earlier, mid-nineteenth-century photographs. They included the mill of the founder of Lewisburg, Ludwig Derr, as well as Lewisburg's nineteenth-century cross-cut canal.

ABOVE John Lee's eighteenth-century stone spring house in Winfield was at or near the site of the last Indian massacre in the county. It still stands near the south side of Main Street, Winfield. This real photo postcard was issued as early as 1907 and in a black- and-white photolithographic version. From the collection of Gary W. and Donna M. Slear.•

TOP LEFT Brown's Mill, Lewisburg, earlier known as Derr's Mill, was photographed in 1860 as a stereo view by photographer James M. Houghton and reissued by Edwin S. Heiser as a real photo postcard prior to 1907. A worker stands in an open doorway. The mill stood near the mouth of Spring Run (later called Limestone or Wilson Run, and finally Bull Run). From the collection of the Union County Historical Society #92.9.91.110.

LEFT The photograph of John Gundy's home (formerly the Penny home and now Lan Avon farm), located at the bend in River Road a mile south of Lewisburg, predates by more than twenty years its issue as a real photo postcard c. 1906. The Gundy farm was frequently visited by Lewisburg and East Buffalo Township residents who purchased milk there. This orchard was also visited, as the *Lewisburg Chronicle*, October 22, 1910, noted, "'Gundy's Orchard Robbed'/Mr. John A. Gundy, who resides just below town, intercepted about a dozen boys who had paid his apple orchard a friendly visit. The boys were not content with taking a few to eat, but had laundry bags full. This is going too far." From the collection of Norman and Peggy Gundy Ulmer.•

Strike Up the Band

Any excuse to decorate with bunting also meant an occasion to strike up the band, and there were many bands formed or forming in towns like Cowan, Swengel, and New Berlin. Postcards of these bands assembling, marching or posed are numerous.

In the first decades of the twentieth century, the celebration of Memorial Day was first and foremost among parades. White Deer, New Berlin, Mifflinburg, and Lewisburg were among the towns hosting parades annually, while services were held at Dreisbach and Ray's Churches. "Memorial Day bunting flags, etc., are being hunted up and brushed off for 30th May display. Let 'Old Glory' have full swing. And above all things else, let the day be sacredly observed," noted the *Mifflinburg Telegraph* on May 25, 1906, as it continued:

The town, everywhere, was in happy holiday attire, "Old Glory" waving resplendent from business and private residences on all the streets, while music from drums, horns, and even gramophones could be heard from early morning until late in the evening. Promptly at 5:30 p.m. the line was formed on Market street by Chief Marshal Jno. T. Hassenplug and Assistant Marshals S. J. Rote and S. B. Hoffman in the following order:

Golden Eagle Band Knights of the Golden Eagle
Crescent Lodge I. O. O. F.
Lewisburg Band
Camp Modern Woodmen
Young Ladies Comprising Decorating
Party
Wm. R. Foster Post and other soldiers

The line of march was down Market to Second St., down Second to Chestnut, up Chestnut to Fifth, up Fifth to Elias Church where details were sent to the different cemeteries and the graves decorated while the band played a dirge. The column then marched to the public stand on the south side of the public school building where nearly 2,000 people had gathered.

ABOVE A band assembles in front of J. F. Groover & Bros. (the cast-iron-front building), west of Donehower's store, near Fifth and Market Streets, Lewisburg, prior to 1915. From the collection of Helen Hopp.•

A Grover Bierly postcard (#40) of the Mifflinburg String Band was taken at the town's Memorial Day parade in 1914. Bierly also photographed the Camp Fire Girls, Flower Girls, and the Boy Scouts as they marched beneath his vantage point. This card is marked "Sample" on the reverse side. From the collection of Gary W. and Donna M. Slear.•

The Mifflinburg String Band, consisting of between twenty and twenty-five players (front row: George Royer, Edgar Rudy, Floyd Boyer, Charles Royer, Warren Gutelius, and Cleve Aumiller; back row: Raymond Beaver, Philip Stahl, Ryan Sechler, Robert Blair, Charles Klingman, Elmer Kempel, Ralph Kleckner, Carl Hassenplug, Frank Dieffenderfer, Ralph Klingman, William Doebler, Horace Barber, Lester Dietrich, Nevin Barnitz, Fred Klose, and Harry Gilbert), was first organized c. 1913. The band was exceedingly popular and played at many events including the large Odd Fellows' parade in Lewisburg, where it was the only string band. World War I decimated its ranks temporarily. The *Mifflinburg Telegraph* of June 24, 1921, announced the band's reorganization and urged its readers, "Let's all get together now and everyone boost the band and the band will be a boost for the town." From the collection of Gary W. and Donna M. Slear.•

A 1914 Grover Bierly photograph shows a crowd assembled in the Mifflinburg Cemetery following the Memorial Day parade and prior to a service at the high school. In the central background is the Old Elias Church near the corner of Green and Fifth Streets, and the cupola of the high school is seen above the trees on the far right. From the collection of the Union County Historical Society #85.7.3.

#40 Mifflinburg String Band, Deco. Day -14

#36 Decoration Day 1914

The Laurel Park Band was photographed in 1906, while the New Berlin Band was photographed after its founding in 1910. •
The New Berlin Silver Cornet Band (1870s) and C. D. Bogar's Brass Band (1880s) were predecessors. Such bands were featured at
fairs, festivals, cake walks, Sunday school picnics, and, of course, parades. From the collection of Gary W. and Donna M. Slear.

RIGHT Three postcards record different aspects of the Odd Fellows' parade held in Lewisburg on April 24, 1914. Flags and
banners ran the length of Market Street. The first card shows the north side of the 400 block of Market Street. A second card shows
the crowd on Market Street (looking east toward Third Street) dressed in spring finery on this April day, and the clock at
curbside advertised Alfred Zeller's jewelry store at 318 Market Street; the banner across the street welcomed Odd Fellows from
sixteen neighboring Central Pennsylvania counties. The third card shows the Berwick Cornet Band as it marched down South
Second Street from Market Street. The correspondent, T. R. Buck, wrote to Walter DeHuff of Glen Rock, York County,
Pennsylvania, "There were about 10,000 in this old town [Lewisburg] that day." From the collections of Joan Sample, Ronald
P. and Beatrice S. Dreese, and the Union County Historical Society #95.1.1. • • •

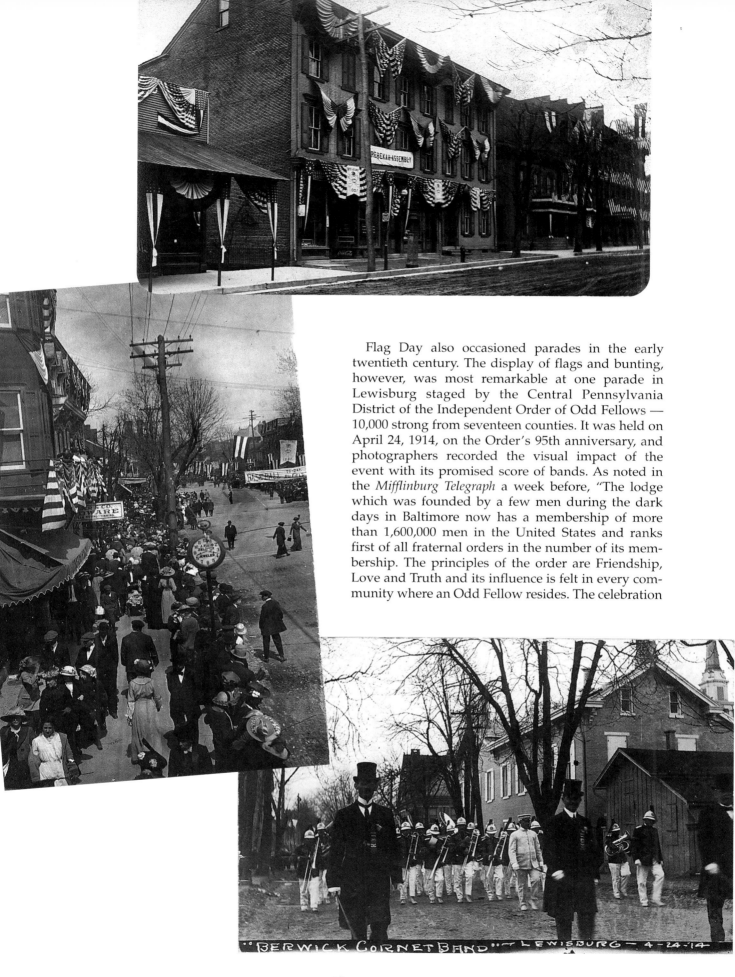

Flag Day also occasioned parades in the early twentieth century. The display of flags and bunting, however, was most remarkable at one parade in Lewisburg staged by the Central Pennsylvania District of the Independent Order of Odd Fellows — 10,000 strong from seventeen counties. It was held on April 24, 1914, on the Order's 95th anniversary, and photographers recorded the visual impact of the event with its promised score of bands. As noted in the *Mifflinburg Telegraph* a week before, "The lodge which was founded by a few men during the dark days in Baltimore now has a membership of more than 1,600,000 men in the United States and ranks first of all fraternal orders in the number of its membership. The principles of the order are Friendship, Love and Truth and its influence is felt in every community where an Odd Fellow resides. The celebration

"BERWICK CORNET BAND" — LEWISBURG — 4-24-14

Home Coming Parade, West Milton, Pa.

No. 2.

WELCOME HOME

Lewisburg, Pa.

HOME COMING
LEWISBURG

in Lewisburg will be an enlightenment to the citizens of the community and to all who are there."[8] Only the World War I homecoming parades — held all over the area in 1919 — came close to equaling the patriotic exuberance and splendor of the Odd Fellows' event.

Devoid of bunting but not of bands or fire equipment were the New Year's Day parades held in Mifflinburg and Lewisburg in the early twentieth century.[9] Mummers, also called "fantastics," were the feature of these parades and distinguished these events from all other parades (as well as the fact that there might well be snow on the ground). As reported of the 1910 Lewisburg event, after twenty-four floats ". . . then came the mummers, in grotesque fashion, marshaled by Charles Stackhouse and Foster Arbogast. There were many funny costumes, good impersonations and plenty of good will throughout the parade."[10] The parade organizers had promised a parade from one to three miles in length with 1,500 marchers from Lewisburg and surrounding towns. Lewisburg repeated the event at least biannually from 1910 through 1916. Like all parades these New Year's Day events had a heavy dose of civic pride and local boosterism:

Lewisburg will usher in the New Year with a monster Mummers' parade which promises to be the largest of its kind ever held in the county seat town. There will be at least three bands in line, upwards of fifty business and industrial floats, as many decorated automobiles, a number of secret societies, fire companies and a long string of fantastics, etc. . . . A number of active committeemen have been at work the last three weeks, and sufficient funds have been raised to offer substantial prizes for the various attractions, such as best floats, the best marching organization, the best comic organization, the best decorated automobile, the tallest and shortest mummer, the best impersonation of Uncle Sam, Maria Pickleweight, hobo, best comic two and four wheeled vehicles, as well as the best original costumed mummer.[11]

The parade formed at two in the afternoon and marched all over town. A band concert and other amusements followed.

January 1, 1916, was also the day when Lewisburg coincidentally celebrated the opening of its newly paved Market Street and the illumination of what the reporter called "the Great White Way."[12] 1916 opened on the note that the region was not looking back but forward — as an area that was prosperous, progressive and growing.[13]

ABOVE   A series of four photographs of a New Year's Day parade in Lewisburg, c. 1910-1916, was made into postcards. The photographer's stationary vantage point looked down on the participants at the northeast corner of South Fourth and Market Streets as they marched east. From the collection of Gary W. and Donna M. Slear.•

LEFT   A World War I Homecoming parade held in 1919 in West Milton featured Mr. Keefer as Uncle Sam. Another Homecoming parade was held in Lewisburg on July 17, 1919. Nelson A. Caulkins took more than two dozen different views of the latter event. John D. Swanger, who photographed the West Milton parade, also took a few shots of the Lewisburg event, which were made into postcards. From the collection of Gary W. and Donna M. Slear.• • •

Come to the Fair

Agriculture has played a key role in Union County since its formation in 1813. The first permanent settlers came to farm its fertile soils — Scots-Irish and Pennsylvania Germans primarily — and they prospered. The Amish, who came from Lancaster, Mifflin, and Berks Counties, also thrived here from c. 1834 to c. 1884; they returned, along with Old Order Mennonites, in even greater numbers in the 1960s.[14]

At the beginning of the twentieth century agricultural production focused on grain crops, while today dairy cattle and poultry are the mainstays. Now, at the close of twentieth century, agriculture remains the major business when judged by the fact that one-third of the county's acreage is still being farmed. Even today, the Amish and Old Order Mennonites still involve their entire families in the planting and harvesting of their crops. Others, such as the Pontius/Wehr/Zimmerman families, having farmed in Buffalo Valley as long as eight generations, now use modern equipment and methods and do not need all family members working on the farm. Many of the postcards from the early twentieth century show families threshing, shocking, working in their fields, or proudly displaying their farm animals.

Farmers formally and competitively began exhibiting their crops and livestock at the first Union County Agricultural Fair, which was held at the county courthouse in New Berlin October 13-14, 1854. Two hundred seventy-five entries were displayed in the commissioners' office and vied for $150 in prize money; cattle were shown in the yard behind the courthouse; a plowing match attracted a crowd. All spectators were admitted free. Jacob Gundy, a successful and progressive farmer in East Buffalo Township, was instrumental in reorganizing the Union County Agricultural Association (founded in 1810) and starting the fair.[15] In 1855 the second fair was extended to three days and held at the University at Lewisburg (Bucknell University) at its Academy (Taylor Hall). The move to the new county seat and the relatively new school was permitted with the provisions that no damage be done to the school and no horses and cattle taken into the woods. Most exhibits were held indoors while the cattle were enclosed in a pen outside. Hartleton was the site of the third fair in the fall of 1856 and

---

ABOVE The Bergenstock residence at Muddy Run, near Mazeppa, serves as a casual portrait of people, livestock, home, and vehicle. An embossed stamp "HALLMAN" was used on the card, which dates from 1907 or later. From the collection of Joseph Prah. •

A farmer from Millmont is posed with his draft horses c. 1909-1911. From the collection of Delphia Shirk. •

A card showing men with their steam engine was sent as a birthday greeting to Barbara Watson in 1912. As late as the mid-1950s, Ollie Hummel from New Berlin brought his steam engine to area farms. The engine drove threshing or other machines by belts, as seen here. From the collection of Jeffrey L. Mensch. •

A man at work during the corn-shocking season was taken by Urs H. Eisenhauer in the western part of Union County c. 1909-1911. From the collection of Delphia Shirk. •

Mifflinburg the site of the fourth in 1857. A temporary exhibit building was erected in both places.

In 1857, the Union County Agricultural Association was incorporated; after another year in temporary quarters (James Dale Chamberlain's farm near Lewisburg), the Association purchased ten acres in East Buffalo Township one mile west of Lewisburg in the area called "Brook Park." The Association paid $150/acre, an amount that some thought outrageously high; but at last the fair had a permanent home, with Bull Run to provide the water supply for the livestock and with room to grow after the purchase of an additional ten acres. In 1859, several large permanent buildings were erected prior to the sixth fair. The Union County Agricultural Association also built a racetrack at the Brook Park site and in 1904 advertised it as being in first-class condition. A new grandstand was ready for occupancy in 1917. At that time the fair lasted four days and had many area bands as entertainment. Train excursions that ran to Brook Park facilitated the trip for the thousands who attended. The fairgrounds became the subject of postcards starting c. 1907.

For the life of the Union County Agricultural Fair (1854-1936) the Association members and promoters aimed to please the public with more and better events: races, bands, contests, and premiums. As noted in the *Lewisburg Chronicle*, September 19, 1908, "This Fair will be Engaging, Exciting, Exhilarating, Enlivening, Enriching, Extensive, Elegant, Educating, Elevating, Excellent, Ennobling, Entertaining, Excelling, Extraordinary, Enterprising, Enticing, Esteemable, Exemplary. Everybody expected, C. Dale Wolfe"; and "Come early. Stay late." However, one mistake may have been in situating the fair so far east in the county because in the late 1920s the West End Fair Committee formed to run its own annual agricultural fair at Lincoln Park in Laurelton.

The Union County Fair's grandstand for viewing horse races was built in 1917, which may be the date of these two views. The two cards form a panorama when placed side by side. The grandstand was demolished in 1937. From the collection of Kenneth A. and Dorothy G. Reish. ••

The Union County Fair, which was held in Brook Park (later called the Auction and now the Farmers' Market), Lewisburg, featured many bands. The Lewisburg Citizens' Band was photographed there as early as 1907. From the collection of the Union County Historical Society #92.9.92.1.

Starting in 1917, produce was sold and displayed at each summer's Anniversary Day on the grounds of the Evangelical Home (United Methodist Homes), Lewisburg. This is one of many photographs taken there by John D. Swanger prior to 1923. From the collection of Gary W. and Donna M. Slear.

Evangelical Home Products.
No. 27   Lewisburg, Pa.

Edwin S. Heiser photographed this pastoral view of the field by River Road just south of the Evangelical Home (Eli Slifer's "Delta Place"), Lewisburg, c. 1907-1922. In contrast to then, today's corn crops are planted very tightly and do not allow the interspersing of pumpkins and squash. From the collection of Joan Sample.•

Apples were a major crop in the area. Here, Oliver Catherman and his daughter, Matilda, stand beside their bushel measures, c. 1918, at his farm in Lewis Township. Other postcards which featured apples include one shown here with "barreled" apples standing beside Beaver Run in Vicksburg as taken by Stephen B. Horton, c. 1907-1911, and another of the orchard of the Zimmerman farm (Sand Run) at the edge of Sugar Valley. Many area farms had orchards, and families made cider and apple butter, and kept their apple harvests in their cellars or an "apple cave" dug in their gardens. From the collections of Harold T. Catherman and Joseph Prah.••

We're Going to Make This Place Really Something

The early twentieth century was an era when individuals, small partnerships, and corporations were often successful in organizing new businesses, such as the Buffalo Valley Telephone Company (est. 1904), electric companies (1907-1911), Central Oaks Heights (1909), Devitt's Camp (1912), and the Evangelical Home (1916); also starting was a new bank, the Lewisburg Trust and Safe Deposit Company (est. 1915), while other banks were renovated: the Union National Bank (1915), the Mifflinburg Bank and Trust Company (1924), and the Lewisburg National Bank (1927). Many churches, such as the Reformed and the Lutheran in Lewisburg, were also being rebuilt or renovated at this time.

The first four decades of the twentieth century would also introduce the county's first large public works: the Laurelton State Village (1917), the Northeastern Federal Penitentiary (1932), and the Federal Courthouse and United States Post Office (1932). Twentieth-century public works differed greatly from those of the nineteenth century. Earlier, entrepreneurs often sought the public's involvement through voluntary association and subscription. For example, in the 1850s the county faced the need of enlarging an older county courthouse in New Berlin or building a new courthouse there or elsewhere. New Berlin did not remain the county seat in large part because not enough funds could be raised by its citizens, while Lewisburg speculators and citizens were more than ready to oblige. Economic prosperity and growth came to Lewisburg at the expense of New Berlin as a result of the relocation of the courthouse, the county's seat.

Private initiative was still essential for the area's progress in the early twentieth century. For example, transforming muddy or rutty dirt walks and roads into "the Great White Way" became a priority for Lewisburg and Mifflinburg citizens in the 1910s and 1920s. The local papers reported, one by one, those individuals who contracted to have their walkways improved with brick or concrete. "Senator [ten-term Congressman] Focht is having a brick pavement put down along the front of his vacant lot on South Second Street," noted the *Lewisburg Chronicle* on June 18, 1904; "The Presbyterian Church authorities have had a nice concrete pavement put down at their parsonage property on Market Street by A. H. Stuck and others," observed the *Mifflinburg Telegraph* on August 6, 1909; while "Dr. A. H. Hill has a fine concrete pavement laid in front of his handsome house on Chestnut Street. His work was done by Isaac F. Stridder and staff of workmen, and is conceded a very elegant piece of work from every standpoint. It is certainly first class in every respect," critiqued the *Mifflinburg Telegraph* on August 30, 1912. Seven hundred feet of cement sidewalks were cast on Market Street, Lewisburg, between May and October 1909. Some citizens were dubious of paving's merits as reflected in the *Lewisburg Chronicle*'s remark, "The Reading Railroad is laying cement pavement on Market Street, beginning at Clark's and across the tracks. There is quite an incline and this winter when the pavements are slippery some one is going to see 'stars.' "

Most people, however, saw the new concrete walks as progress and followed suit with streets and roads. In 1915 Lewisburg covered its entire Market Street with bricks over concrete. In 1920, Mifflinburg covered its dirt Chestnut Street with concrete one block at a time, at a cost of $1.43 a yard.[16]

Other parts of the county followed the lead of its two largest boroughs. The Buffalo Valley Good Roads Association was formed in 1929 to encourage the county commissioners to secure state moneys for other roads by utilizing an existing state government program[17] which matched local funds three to one for paving projects. In 1929 a new state-financed road from Allenwood to Dewart was constructed, and the state highway department announced plans for construction of a new concrete road between Winfield and the Evangelical Home just north of Lewisburg, a distance in excess of five miles. The new road rerouted the traffic which previously went into Lewisburg via River Road onto a new bypass just west of Bucknell's stadium. This bypass utilized Ninth Street west of the new Lewisburg High School and went over both the Pennsylvania and the Reading railroads' tracks. New Berlin sought to have a macadam road constructed between it and Winfield. Pressure also came from the White Deer Motor Club in 1931 to have a proper road connect White Deer to the White Deer/Watsontown bridge. Dirt roads were considered relics which did not have a place in a truly progressive era. Real photo postcards recorded some of this progress.

Other improvements included the introduction of telephone service by the Home Telephone Company in 1895, followed by rapid expansion of communications under the Buffalo Valley Telephone Company, which was established in 1904 with $10,000 in local capital.[18] The phone directories went from a single sheet to a slim volume with nearly 300 phones by 1905. In an article, "Telephones for the Farms," the point was made:

Truly this is the age of progress. What is commonplace to the present generation was undreamed of by their grandsires. Event upon event, and improvement upon improvement have come with such startling rapidity that even those

A major flood in 1865 destroyed Lewisburg's first wooden bridge (opened in 1818). Shortly afterward, the Lewisburg Bridge Company, a private corporation, built a new covered toll bridge about 400 feet to the north, near St. John Street. This bridge was used by pedestrians, buggies, and wagons as well as trains. It sustained damage in the 1889 "Johnstown" flood. Started in 1906, a new steel bridge for cars and pedestrians was built near the site of the town's first bridge, and in 1912 a steel railroad and trolley bridge was built on the piers of the 1865 toll bridge. The construction of the vehicular/pedestrian bridge as captured in this card includes the steam-powered hoisting equipment. From the collection Kenneth A. and Dorothy G. Reish. •

In 1905 the former toll house stood at the eastern end of Market Street, Lewisburg. Long obsolete, it had been converted into a home, but it blocked access to the proposed new free bridge. The house was auctioned off for $56.50 and subsequently moved to its present location at the southwest corner of North Water and St. Anthony Streets. The toll house is seen on this card dating before 1907, flanked by the Lewisburg Water Company, its water towers or "stand pipes" (only their bases remain today), and the Irland house (barely visible on the right). From the collection of the Union County Historical Society #92.9.91.154.

Paving of the 300 block on Lewisburg's Market Street in 1914 was photographed and reproduced as several postcards by Edwin S. Heiser. The photographs were taken looking west. The top view shows a steamroller compacting a thick layer of sand and gravel on the north side of the street, while the second view shows a team of horses grading the dirt street on the south side. A sign advertises Alpha Cement, and a large pile of paving bricks is evident. Recent core samples show that the bricks were set into a layer of concrete. The cost was $2.12 a square yard. From the collection of Joan Sample.••

BOTTOM The paving of South Third Street, Mifflinburg, was photographed c. 1921. From the collection of Jeffrey L. Mensch.

fully abreast of the times, have to gasp with surprised admiration. The telephone, which, after all, has only had its development in recent years, is a greater boon to farmers than to any other class of people.[19]

Electricity came to Lewisburg in 1907. The smaller crossroads communities and homes in the countryside, however, would lag behind the county seat and Mifflinburg by eighteen or more years. It was not until 1925 that Winfield "…had the joy of using electricity for the first time last Tuesday evening [January 5]. After many days of waiting, the current was furnished by the Pennsylvania Power & Light Company of Sunbury. The town presented a fine appearance and needless to say the residents were 'quite excited.'"[20] Gas fixtures were slowly replaced by electric light bulbs, sometimes seen hanging at street intersections in the local postcards. Laurelton got street lights on poles in 1929 — an expense paid for by its residents.

As much a part of "keeping up" as the embrace of new technologies were the formation of civic clubs and the organization of town cleanups.[21] Mifflinburg promoted a town cleanup as an annual May event starting in 1916, as part of "National Clean Up Week." In the April 21, 1916, edition the town paper noted, "In a very short time Nature will be doing her share to make Mifflinburg more beautiful but nature cannot clean up your back yard or haul ground, ashes, and rubbish to the dump. Will you do your share to make this town clean? Many other towns are taking up this work and profiting by it." The town council promised to haul away all that was brought to the alleys during the annual spring cleaning — and still does.

Individual home improvements were also enumerated in the newspapers. "Dr. Chs. H. Gutelius has had a fine stone pavement located in front of his pretty home, which home or house he had recently repainted white with green shutters, making a very nice appearance;" "Mr. John W. Gutelius painted his handsome and modern home on Green Street. It certainly looks fine and the workmanship and blending of colors are very artistic and beautiful"; and "Mr. Harry Wilkinson is having a nice porch erected at his house on Walnut Street," noted the *Mifflinburg Telegraph* on May 26, 1905, and July 14, 1905. Homes like these were often the subject of postcards that served as "portraits."

Institutions were also expanding their services or developing new ones at this time. In 1916 the Central Pennsylvania Conference of the United Evangelical Church purchased the Eli Slifer mansion just north of Lewisburg to create a home for their aged parishioners and the orphans of Evangelical families. The Conference began by converting the twenty-room mansion, its two farm houses, and outbuildings. Later, new buildings including the Orphanage were constructed. As a local paper noted, "This is an advanced step taken by the Evangelical denomination. A more ideally located plot of land for such an institution could not be found anywhere in the State. The buildings are on a moderately high hill, overlooking the Susquehanna river and the beautiful and fertile Buffalo Valley …There is an abundance of fruit on the land, while the mansion is surrounded by beautiful trees and shubbery."[22]

Earlier, the Evangelical Central Pennsylvania Conference had established the Central Oaks Heights camp meeting ground on a promontory just south of West Milton (formerly the site of Oneida Chief Shikellamy's headquarters and now the Bethesda Center). A tabernacle at which 2,000 people could assemble for Bible study in a relaxed summertime environment was erected in 1909. Central Oak Heights was patterned on well-established summer religious communities like Ocean Grove, New Jersey, and Oak Bluffs on Martha's Vineyard, Massachusetts.[23] Central Oak Heights provided a permanent home to the Central Pennsylvania Bible Conference Society (comprised of Centre, Clinton, Lycoming, Columbia, Montour, and Northumberland Counties). "The fine large tabernacle is probably not surpassed by any similar building in the State. The boarding hall and dormitory, situated on the Ridge Avenue promenade afford an enchanting outlook, both northward and southward that makes the dining hour a great delight," remarked the *Mifflinburg Telegraph*, September 18, 1909. In addition there were boarding houses, cottages, and tents. In 1910 the rates for board were modest: single breakfasts or suppers were 25 cents each and dinners were 50 cents; $7.50 paid for the entire season of forty meals, with preachers being given reduced rates. The tabernacle had electricity, and a phone was installed on the grounds within a year. Both Central Oak Heights and the Evangelical Home were the subject of many cards, as was Devitt's Camp.

A physician from Philadelphia, Dr. William Devitt, opened a treatment center for tuberculosis patients in a converted barn on the northern slope of White Deer Mountain, southwest of Allenwood, in 1912. Within six years Devitt's "Camp" expanded from an attending

A series of at least nine shots was taken by Millmont photographer Urs H. Eisenhauer, c. 1910, when sections of the Old Turnpike (formerly a toll road between Lewisburg and Mifflinburg) were being graded and paved. Another card, not part of the Eisenhauer series, shows the apparatus for heating tar as it stood in Vicksburg during the paving of the Turnpike. From the collection of Gary W. and Donna M. Slear, and Joseph Prah. ••••

Entrance Gate

Central Oak Heights, West Milton, Pa, No. 3.
Swarey Photo

Central Oak Heights
West Milton, Pa.
No. 5.
Swarey Photo

Many real photo postcards were made of Central Oak Heights, the Evangelical Church's camp meeting ground, from its opening in the summer of 1909 until c. 1944. These five views show its entrance from Route 15 just south of West Milton; the view south toward the river from the top of the Heights; the tents as they looked in the summer months; the Tabernacle; and the Hornberger Cottage. All but the first were taken by John D. Swanger, a Milton photographer, who took many shots there c. 1909-1923. From the collections of the Union County Historical Society #89.15.6, Gary W. and Donna M. Slear, and Janice C. Dreese.

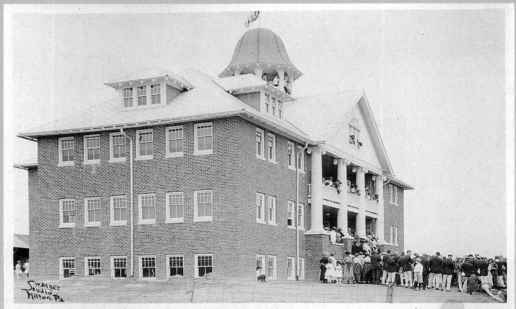

In April 1916 the Evangelical Home (United Methodist Homes), Lewisburg, for the aged and orphans of Evangelicals was established at the former home of Eli Slifer. The Central Conference purchased the property from Dr. Lamont H. Ross for $30,000. The card shows how the property looked at the time of the purchase. From the collection of Ronald P. and Beatrice S. Dreese.•

A postcard, c. 1921, shows the Orphanage, a building which still stands close to the railroad tracks on the west side of the property. It is one of a number of real photo postcards issued by John D. Swanger of the Evangelical Home. From the collection of Gary W. and Donna M. Slear.

RIGHT The approach to Devitt's Camp, Allenwood, as it appeared betwen 1912 and1923, was one of sixteen different views produced by John D. Swanger of Milton. A second card is titled, " 'Service men' at Devitt's Camp July 4, 1921" and shows a nurse with some patients. The third person from the left in the back row is Spry Arthur Sparks, who was from the Philadelphia area. From the collection of the Union County Historical Society #96.1.1-.2.•

local physician and a manager to a larger staff and numerous cottages housing thirty patients. The U.S. Public Health Bureau and the Veterans' Bureau sent disabled servicemen there at the end of World War I, doubling the camp's patient load. In 1923 the facility had a modern sanitorium and 128 patients. With the help of civic and church groups like the "Workers for Devitt" from St. Peter's Reformed Church in Kelly Township, and with the management of a strong superintendent, Herbert Norton, Dr. Devitt succeeded in creating a much-needed health institution.[24]

Trains and trolleys remained private ventures in the 1900s, but roads and bridges became public enterprises. Road paving in particular was promoted by Pennsylvania's Governor Pinchot in the 1920s,[25] while local politicians like G. C. Mohn and Benjamin Focht promoted the region, making sure this part of Central Pennsylvania got its fair share of growing state and federal budgets. The so-called "free bridges" were instead paid for by state and local governments — from taxpayer dollars.[26]

Other large public works followed the construction of the new steel bridges. State and federal moneys were involved in establishing institutions new to the county: the Laurelton State Village for Feeble-Minded Women of Child-Bearing Age[27] and the Northeastern Federal Penitentiary in Lewisburg. The former was the result of social legislation initiated at the state level by the state's Federation of Women's Clubs and the State Board of Public Charities, as well as state and county medical societies.

The Laurelton project was begun in 1913 with a modest state appropriation of $50,000, a site in state forest, and the donation of 217 privately-owned acres at the foot of the Seven Mile Narrows north of Laurelton. Four years later, the *Mifflinburg Telegraph* noted on March 2, 1917, "The site chosen is close to the geographical centre of the state, yet sufficiently isolated to permit of the proper handling of the institution of this type apart from the gaze of curious spectators …A splendid range of hills encloses the site on the north and provides a bountiful supply of pure mountain water …Fine building stone is found in abundance for the construction of the buildings." After many delays by the state legislature, the first stone "cottage" was occupied by thirty-six patients in 1919 — a far cry from the 2,400 patients initially envisioned. However, ten years later there were 700 patients living and working in a dozen buildings on 1,000 acres. It was the largest institution of its type in Pennsylvania, but not one without trials and tribulations. As its methods

"Service men" at Devitt's Camp July 4th 1921

Arthur R. Ishiguro took photographs of the exterior of the Laurelton State Village as well as its sewing and laundry rooms c. 1924. From the collection of the Union County Historical Society #92.9.89.3 and #86.3.16. ••

RIGHT Two extant postcards show the first forty-three federal prisoners as they arrived at the train station in Montandon on November 14, 1932, from the Atlanta Penitentiary. The men were transferred to the prison in buses as shown in these photographs and noted in the *Mifflinburg Telegraph* three days later: "The transfer was effected under heavy police guard without disorder or difficulty of any kind. Two buses of the West Branch Bus Company were waiting at the station, along with a squad of highway patrolmen from the Milton detail. The prisoners were marched in single file from the front end of the coach to the waiting buses." From the collection of the Union County Historical Society #93.10.1. •

Several real photo postcards illustrated the Northeastern Federal Penitentiary, Lewisburg. This card has the opening date of November 14, 1932, on its front. Linen cards of the penitentiary were issued later. From the collection of Ronald Nornhold. •

and administration changed over the decades, the institution was renamed the Laurelton State School (1962). It was not unusual to see many of its residents visiting or working at homes in the local communities, and the Laurelton State School (now called Laurelton Center) continues to be the largest employer in Hartley Township.

The building of a federal correctional institution in Union County was as anxiously awaited as the Laurelton Village had been earlier — and the subject of a few cards as well. The *Mifflinburg Telegraph* announced on August 7, 1930, "Union County Site Selected for New Federal Penitentiary." One thousand twenty-four acres — ten productive farms — were purchased two and one-half miles north of Lewisburg, four miles west of Milton, and, as far as others were concerned, in the middle of nowhere. The accompanying article noted, "Modern methods of dealing with crime is to get criminals away from the congestion of cities, and into the cleaner environment of the open country." The expenditure of nearly $100,000 for the land and $3,500,000 for the facility's construction was welcome news during the Great Depression, as was the prison's payroll. From December 1930, when an architect's drawing was published and bids solicited, until the open house for 42,142 people in mid-November 1932, the penitentiary was frequently mentioned in the local press. Not the least was the news:

The Great Lakes Construction Company of Chicago, contractors for the Northeastern Penitentiary to be built near Lewisburg commenced work today. Walter Landin of Chicago will superintend operations at the site of the penitentiary. He is making his headquarters at the Cameron House, Lewisburg. Only six men will be sent from Chicago by the Great Lakes Company. They will be the time-keeper and the following foremen: carpenter, labor, electrical, plumbing, cement work, and stone and brick work. All other labor will be hired from around here.[28]

PX AND RECREATION HALL — 1394TH CO. C.C.C. (VET) WEIKERT, PA.

INTERIOR OF BARRACKS

From 1933 to 1942, the Civilian Conservation Corps was involved in the county in extensive reforestation efforts, bridge and trail building, road maintenance, as well as the construction of masonry structures such as the dam and bath pavilion at Rapid Run (Raymond B. Winter State Park). There were several CCC camps in Union County: one was near Bear Run Road (the Joyce Kilmer Camp), one near Livonia (the Halfway Camp), and one less than a mile east of Weikert (the Bald Eagle Camp). Interior views were taken of the latter, the 1394th Co. Civilian Conservation Corps' PX/Recreation Hall and Barracks (one of three) in Weikert (the former Brungard farm and presently the Union County Sportsmen Club on Hassenplug Road). It was a CCC camp exclusively for older men, veterans of World War l. The Bald Eagle Camp began with fifty to sixty men and had as many as one hundred at its peak. From the collection of the Union County Historical Society #92.9.89.5-.6. ••

We're on the Move: Trains, Buggies and Cars

Just as trails or waterways had earlier been essential to the area's economic and cultural growth, easy access to "the iron horse" became crucial to the region's success and development from the mid-nineteenth century on.[29] Towns declined or prospered as a result of their ability to use political muscle and raise the necessary capital to attract train service. For example, when Lewisburg secured access to the Lewisburg, Centre & Spruce Creek Railroad (Pennsylvania Railroad) in 1869, it gained the advantage over former commercial centers like New Berlin and, temporarily, Mifflinburg (which saw the line extended to it in 1871). Much was at stake, and individuals like John Walls and Eli Slifer made their fortunes at this time. As the twentieth century dawned, parts of Union County were still struggling for that access. The pressure not to be left behind in an increasingly fast-paced world was more evident than ever. It is therefore not surprising that many postcards featured trains and local stations.

Trains were instrumental in the rise of new hamlets like Vicksburg, Swengel, Millmont, Laurel Park, and Glen Iron — towns which were comprised of twenty to forty homes, a store or two, and churches — which formed around farmers' freight depots. West Milton grew from an insignificant crossroads community into a full-fledged town as a result of the construction there of the Philadelphia & Reading (later, Reading Company) Railroad's roundhouse. In contrast, the late establishment of a train line could cause economic stagnation as it did at New Berlin, the former cultural center and county seat. New Berlin's attempts to acquire rail service illustrated the hopes and frustrations of other small towns like Hartleton and Laurelton, which had previously thrived due to their location on major roads but which lost out when train routes were selected.[30] Some villages were bypassed by only of a mile or two. Other small towns like Mazeppa, White Springs, and Dice remained so — neither made nor broken in the rail era.

Buggies continued to provide light and relatively inexpensive transportation for America's rural families. Buggies became especially important to the prosperity of Union County when Mifflinburg became a major manufacturer of them from 1865 to 1915, producing more per capita than any other town in Pennsylvania.[31]

The early decades of the twentieth century saw the introduction of the automobile and its change from rare curiosity to widespread usage. In 1909, Samuel Grove sagely observed in his column, "Jottings," in the *Mifflinburg Telegraph*, "The foresighted buggy maker considers the signs of the times and betakes himself to auto making."[32]

ABOVE "The R. R. Station of White Deer was burglarously entered on last Saturday night, but nothing of value was secured save the agent's brier pipe," reported the *Mifflinburg Telegraph*, March 31, 1905. The *Lewisburg Chronicle* later reported on October 23, 1909, "Last Sunday morning, about half past one o'clock, a southbound freight crew discovered the station at White Deer on fire. The train was stopped and the crew broke open the door and saved the ticket case and one or two barrels of freight. The building and everything else was burned, including a new typewriter and some personal effects of the agent, W. S. Dreisbaugh . . . It has been broken into a number of times by thieves during the past seven years, since the abolition of the night service, and some incline to the belief that the building was robbed and then set on fire to hide evidence of the crime. It is known that boat loads of thieves go up the river and rob farmers of fruit, grain, vegetables and poultry." The old freight station was refitted for temporary service in the meantime. The interior view of the new passenger station, completed in 1911, was photographed by Mary Barber Hagey in 1912 and shows her father, Frank Elias Barber, and her sister, Alice. Two different exterior views of the station were issued, and one was included in a composite real photo postcard of White Deer. From the collection of Betty Hagey Herald.•

The notation, "Pennsylvania & Reading Cut, Milton, PA," is misleading since the views were taken before 1907 at the West Milton tower near the steel bridge which crossed the Susquehanna River from West Milton to Milton. The P. & R. Catawissa Branch forks to the left and goes over the bridge while the double track line to the right goes to Lewisburg. From the collection of Gary W. and Donna M. Slear.

Views of the engine house in West Milton and some of its crew (including Mr. Reitmeyer, second from left) were taken in 1907 or later. West Milton was a bustling railroad town from 1901 until 1940. Seventy-five men were employed there as train gangs, yard men, coal dock men, air men, oilers, and telegraphers. An average of seventeen to nineteen passenger trains in addition to freight trains were serviced there each day. From the collection of Gary W. and Donna M. Slear.••

From 1898 to 1928 an electric-operated trolley car ran between Watsontown, Milton, and Lewisburg. In the early years, the trolley went only as far as the Montandon side of Lewisburg's wooden toll bridge as seen in the top view (a bench on the left and a shelter on the right were at the end of the line). The close-up view of the toll bridge includes a sign which reads: "Attend/The Great Fair/1906/Lewisburg/four days/September 25 to 28." At that date, passengers would have had to go over the bridge as pedestrians, some of whom are seen in the second card. The third card shows a trolley emerging on the Lewisburg side in 1911. Then, as noted in the *Lewisburg Chronicle* of January 14, 1911, " . . .one can board the cars at the Pensy [*sic*] station instead of walking across the river bridge. . ." A year later the trolley was extended west to Mifflinburg. From the collections of the Union County Historical Society #92.9.91.160,.162, and Joan Sample.• • •

Pennsylvania Station

The Pennsylvania Railroad passenger and freight station (built in 1869) was located at the southwest corner of North Second and St. John Streets, Lewisburg. This rail line (initially called the Lewisburg, Centre & Spruce Creek Railroad, later the Lewisburg & Tyrone Railroad) ran west through the county. Another view shows the Baker House, which was adjacent to the station on North Second Street (parking lot for Cole's Hardware). The locomotive is a Pennsy class H3. The second photograph was taken by Edwin S. Heiser, and it includes the barber shop which stood until the late 1960s behind the former Lentz/Troutman Pharmacy (Shoemaker Gallery) at the corner of Market and Second Streets. The Baker House (first a hotel and then an apartment house) was razed in 1962 and the station razed in 1963. Both cards date from c. 1906. From the collection of the Union County Historical Society #92.9.90.25 and #92.9.91.101.•

TOP RIGHT A train is seen pulling away from the Vicksburg station in a card produced by Stephen B. Horton c. 1907-1911. From the collection of Joseph Prah.•

RIGHT The enlarged and improved Mifflinburg passenger/freight depot was featured on this card sent in 1914 by Mrs. Q. P. Roadarmel to Mr. Francis Moll in Millmont. "We expect too [sic] have a bean spelling gathering this coming Wed. eve. if ugly Thurs. eve. Be sure & bring your sweethearts & come. Don't disappoint us please," wrote Mrs. Roadarmel. For several years the citizens had petitioned the railroad for a new depot. " . . . we have but a poor excuse of a R. R. station, really a disgrace to the Company as well as to Mifflinburg . . . Almost daily it is so crowded that passengers are compelled to stand or to seek the platform outside. It is also unsanitary, caused by the nearby toilet room, which is unfit for use," noted the *Mifflinburg Telegraph*, November 25, 1910. The west bound train for Bellefonte is probably a D14 class. From the collection of Billy and Lindy Mattern.

RIGHT Ida from Weikert, Union County, wrote her friend, Mrs. M. P. Shrader of Selinsgrove, Snyder County, in 1907, "Your postcard rec'd was very glad to hear from you I wish you could surprise me like this post card This is Cherry Run bridge the old one. The new one isn't finished." The view is titled on the card's front, "Scene along the L. & T. R. R. [Lewisburg & Tyrone Railroad, in Hartley Township]." From the collection of Ronald Nornhold.•

P.R.R. Station, Vicksburg, Pa.   Horton Photo

P.R.R. DEPOT

Scene along the L. & T. R. R.

ABOVE The Philadelphia & Reading Railroad (later Reading) passenger station on South Fifth Street, Lewisburg (built in 1882/1883), as it appeared on a card sent in 1908. It was the second rail line (initially called the Shamokin, Sunbury & Lewisburg Railroad) to enter the county, and it ran along the county's eastern edge from Winfield to Allenwood and on to Williamsport and Newberry, Lycoming County. The Lewisburg station was the envy of others as the *Mifflinburg Telegraph* remarked on November 25, 1910, "Take our neighboring town of Lewisburg: they have a two apartment station, with telegraph office on the second floor, baggage room separate, with an employee for just that purpose." Only the freight station remains standing; the passenger station was razed in 1954. Another Reading station was in New Columbia and photographed by Stephen B. Horton. • The card was sent "From one brother [Warren] to another [Foster Ranck in New Columbia]" on November 23, 1907. On the side of the station is an advertisement for Lucas Paints. Along with a large graphic hand are the words: "Rub your finger in pure white lead. Several months old it comes off like chalk." From the collection of Gary W. and Donna M. Slear.

RIGHT The passenger train station at West Milton as it appeared prior to 1907. Fourteen posters advertise Bank's Business College, Acker's Bon Bons, Mennen's Toilet Powder, and Coca Cola, among other items. From the collection of the Union County Historical Society #86.3.17.

RIGHT The train station in Millmont had more photographs taken of it than any other station in Union County. Its peony beds were captured in full bloom in a 1906 card written "hastily" to Miss Marion Stover of Aaronsburg from Mame Hoffman. The Ruhl & Watson box factory is seen on the right. From the collection of Ronald P. and Beatrice S. Dreese. •

RIGHT The New Berlin & Winfield narrow gauge steam line was featured in two different real photo postcards. Its six-ton engine was photographed leaving its shed in New Berlin before 1907, as shown here, and at the Winfield station in 1910. The line included a passenger coach and a number of freight and coal cars. Trains ran between New Berlin and Winfield from 1905 to 1916. However, the traffic on the line was not enough to sustain any reversals like the washouts of the summer of 1912. The line went into receivership at that time and finally closed. From the collection of Donald F. Kline.

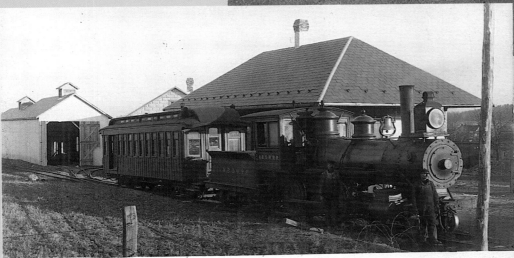

U.H. EISENHAUER, PHOTO

Rapidly embraced as *the* form of transportation by the average American, the automobile signaled the demise of the buggy era and with it the decline of Mifflinburg as an important commercial center. The first automobile in Union County was sighted in Mifflinburg on July 29, 1901, followed by the county's first auto registrations in 1903. While photographs and postcards in the following years continued to show people in their buggies, local people were increasingly photographed in cars. The former Mifflinburg Body and Gear plant at Green and North Eighth Streets converted in 1916 to making truck bodies, then station wagons and, finally, trailers. In 1928 it was still thriving and in fact accounted for half of the town's payroll; four years later, however, through a combination of factors, the Mifflinburg Body and Gear's last station wagon rolled off the line, and in 1941 the former buggy works went bankrupt.

Not until the 1960s, with the influx of Old Order Mennonites and Amish from Lancaster County, did buggies again become part of the area's transportation system. By that time trains were also merely a curiosity for the tourist or reserved for an occasional freight run.

ABOVE Dreese Moyer posed in his buggy for Millmont photographer Urs H. Eisenhauer, c. 1909-1911, probably in the western end of Union County where both lived. Grover Bierly's postcard of the home of hardware store owners Robert and Magaret Snodgrass on 278 Market Street, Mifflinburg, shows what might have been their first car c. 1914-1917. From the collections of Delphia Shirk and Katherine Roush.•

TOP RIGHT Samuel K. Strickler and his family were photographed when they went for a ride in their crimson Dusenberg c. 1914. It was one of the first automobiles owned by a Mifflinburg resident. Strickler was prosperous at the time, owning a home on Chestnut and Fifth Streets, six double houses on Walnut Street between Fifth and Sixth Streets, and the former David Kauffman farm in West Buffalo Township. He also owned and operated a food stock business until 1927. From the collection of J. Randall Chambers.•

Mr. and Mrs. Oscar Bowersox were out for a ride in Millmont when they were photographed by Urs H. Eisenhauer, c.1909-1911, while Dr. Oliver Wendell Holmes Glover of Laurelton posed with his Model T Ford (often called a "tin lizzie" or "flivver") in front of his drug store and the office of Dr. Mohn in 1912. From the collections of Delphia Shirk • and the Union County Historical Society #88.21.8.

Δ Θ Ψ House Lewisburg, Pa.

ABOVE Across from the president's house at Bucknell University was Loomis Field and the hill with Old Main at its crest. Various events were held on the field and hillside including open-air concerts, football games, the annual class rush, or a reading of "As You Like It," seen here with Tustin Gym in the left background. These outdoor events predated the construction of Bucknell's stadium in 1924 and a theatre in 1959. The postcard dates from as early as 1907 and is one of two views taken of the performance. From the collection of the Union County Historical Society #92.9.91.11.

Among several views of the annual Bucknell University class rush of September 19, 1908, one shows the sophomores poised for action while another shows the freshmen dragging sophomores over the sophomore line. The sequence of photographs creates a feeling of movement and turmoil. From the collection of the Union County Historical Society #85.19.1-.4 and #92.9.92.118.

Bucknell University N.J.

The Star

Bucknell University N.J.

The rush Freshmen draging the
Sophomores over the line
Sept. 19 190

Bucknell
ru

in 1917 when the Centre Point, Feese, Grove, Lincoln, Pike, and Pine Schools in Hartley Township closed to form the Hartleton Elementary School. In 1930, just before most of the one-room schools began closing, forty-seven of them were operating in Union County. At that time, twenty-two of the teachers were women and five of them were married.[36] When the Amish and Old-Order Mennonites began coming into the area in the 1960s, they used former schools which had not been converted into auxiliary farm buildings or homes. Only a few one-room schools remain empty today.

This period also brought the creation of libraries for the public's benefit. The first to be built was the William D. Himmelreich Memorial Library of the First Presbyterian Church in Lewisburg in 1902. As the *Lewisburg Chronicle* remarked on December 24, 1910, "This library, comprising about 4,400 volumes of choice books, has now been made free to all resi-

dents of Lewisburg …The reading room with its reference library and its papers and magazines, nearly thirty in number, has always been open to the public. The issuing of books will begin with the new year, but the library will be open December 28-31 to give opportunity for the issuing of application cards." Subsequently, the Herr Memorial Library was established in Mifflinburg (1934), followed by small community libraries later in Vicksburg (1948) and in Laurelton (1979). In 1989, the use and space need had long outgrown the Himmelreich building in Lewisburg, and residents from all over the county mounted a major capital campaign to build a new library in the Brook Park area, calling it the Public Library for Union County. The Himmelreich Library is now used as a sectarian reading room.

Church life has always been an integral part of the community. The Lutheran, German Reformed

The interior of the William D. Himmelreich Library and Reading Room was taken in 1907 when it was furnished in the craftsman style of the period. The library was built adjacent to the First Presbyterian Church on Market Street, Lewisburg. From the collection of Gary W. and Donna M. Slear.•

Three churches in Lewisburg were razed since they were photographed in the early twentieth century. The Lutheran Church at 100 South Third Street was razed prior to 1902; in the background is the cupola of the Benjamin Focht home (the Tuscan Villa) and the side of the Union County Courthouse, both on South Second Street.• The Congregational Christian Church on North Third Street (now site of the Heritage House) was built in 1854 and razed in 1963. The United Evangelical Church at 42 South Fourth Street was built in 1861 and razed in 1915 (renamed St. Paul's United Methodist Church). From the collections of Joan Sample and Gary W. and Donna M. Slear.

(United Church of Christ), Evangelical, Presbyterian, and Methodist denominations were the most prevalent in the early history of the county and continued thus into the early decades of the twentieth century.[37] The Baptist Church in Lewisburg had strong ties to Bucknell well into the twentieth century. Other groups like the plain sect Dunkards and Amish had smaller numbers in the area. The Roman Catholics had been part of Lewisburg's early history but had declined until a large influx of Catholics at the time the Penitentiary was built made construction of the Sacred Heart Catholic Church in Lewisburg a reality in 1935.

Early postcards exist of most of the area's churches, and a few cards show their interiors. In the period 1905-1935, many of the larger congregations were meeting in their second or third building, sometimes located at or near their first site.

63 CHRISTIAN CHURCH LEWISBURG, PA.

93 United Evangelical Church, Lewisburg.

Washington Presbyterian Church.

Also razed were the Washington Presbyterian Church (built in 1830), Gregg Township, photographed c. 1908; and the Dreisbach Church, Buffalo Township, which had its exterior and interior photographed by Stephen B. Horton c. 1907-1911. The United Evangelical Church (Trinity United Methodist), New Columbia, was a wooden structure built in 1843 and remodeled with a brick veneer in 1927 after its exterior and interior were taken in 1908. •• From the collections of Gary W. and Donna M. Slear, Joseph Prah, and Charles and Patricia Longley.

1908 U. Ev. Childrens Day, New Columbia, Pa.

United Ev. Church New Columbia, Pa. Horton Photo

Dreisbach Church, Buffalo Valley, Pa. Horton Photo.

Interior Dreisbach S.S. Room,
Buffalo Valley, Pa.
Horton Photo.

Interior Dreisbach Church, Buffalo Valley, Pa. Horton Photo.

West Milton, Pa.

Main St. Harlleton Pa

White Deer Pa

Taking in the Town

At the dawn of this era, on November 16, 1908, "W," a former resident of Union County, wrote to the editor of the *Lewisburg Chronicle* from his home in Minneapolis, Minnesota:

During my absence of fifty years I have visited Lewisburg at long intervals and on all such occasions it rather saddened my heart to see how Lewisburg (my native place and still affectionately remembered) had lagged behind and had really lost its place in the procession. From a business standpoint it lost ground, and it might just as well have been fenced in years ago and kept as a hunting preserve for very small game. I would walk over brick pavements laid in the early part of the last century — all gullied out and disfigured by use — curbing on the streets standing at all angles — residences untidy and partially dismantled, a general appearance — outside limited areas — of decay and dry rot. This same spirit of listlessness and indifference seemed to pervade the surrounding country.... This is an age of progress and people more and more love the beautiful, but what have the Lewisburg people done to idealize this growing sentiment for the beautiful? ...Of course, as a quiet, peaceful place to sleep the long sleep of death — awaiting the resurrection day, Lewisburg is to be commended. Therefore, wake up, and go forward.

Were towns like Lewisburg as sleepy and run-down as the writer said? Was "W" exaggerating to make his point in support of the town's Civic Club and its beautification efforts even stronger?

No matter one's point of view on what "the look" of progress in rural America should be, real photo postcard views of the area's towns captured what was there. Some cards were composites which tried to include as many visual images as possible. Crossroads villages like Forest Hill and Dry Valley might have only one view made of them, while larger towns like Lewisburg and Mifflinburg were portrayed on dozens if not several hundred different cards.

Professionals and semi-professionals like Grover Bierly, Urs H. Eisenhower, and Stephen B. Horton benefited from the public's appreciation of their cards. Horton, a "commercial traveler," not only sold biscuits to the local shopkeepers in Laurelton, Swengel, Hartleton, Vicksburg, Buffalo Cross Roads, Forest Hill, and Montandon but also returned to sell the postcards he developed. Horton's postcards served as portraits of the stores and some of the local customers, providing a visual representation of this era in rural American life.

Real photo postcards tended to present the more modern homes, like that of Philip and Nell Linn (built 1901/1902), not the older homes like that of the McClures further down University Avenue. Streetscapes and "bird's-eye" views cast an even broader, more generalized view of the rural towns. Only Mary Barber Hagey's casual shot of sheep in her front yard in White Deer might indicate the contradictions of town living at that time — a scene "W," a Union Countian turned city slicker, possibly found offensive rather than picturesque. Ordinances banning the raising of sheep, pigs, cows, or chickens in the towns like White Deer or Lewisburg were not yet in place.[38]

TOP LEFT Numerous "bird's-eye" views were taken of Mifflinburg by John C. Slear, Maurice E. Royer, and Grover Bierly. In comparison, fewer panoramas exist of Allenwood and West Milton (Datesman's Station). Here the photographer was situated on a hill north of West Milton, looking south towards the Susquehanna River and the road to Lewisburg. From the collection of Gary W. and Donna M. Slear.

The card of Main Street, Hartleton, faces east toward the roads leading to Mifflinburg on the left (Route 45) and to Millmont on the right. The orientation of the roads, c. 1907, including the incline, has remained the same. From the collection of Delphia Shirk.

A composite real photo postcard produced by M. L. Zercher B. & S. Co. of Topeka, Kansas, in 1913, includes a "bird's-eye" view of White Deer (previously called Hightown), the Reading Railroad train station, a streetscape, and the main square, all taken by John D. Swanger c. 1911-1912. From the collection of Gary W. and Donna M. Slear.

The White Deer Flour Mill, operated by Jerome Hornberger, is shown here with workers, customers, a large Fairbanks scale in the opening on the extreme right, and a delivery wagon from Diehl's Bakery in Watsontown c. 1906. The mill closed in 1928 after a destructive fire. The sign for the White Deer Inn in the foreground reminds one of the occasional sightings of albino deer. "Last Friday the members of Larry's Creek Hunting and Fishing Club shot the largest buck yet reported this season. He was a big albino, being pure white with the exception of a few brown spots along the back," mentioned the *Lewisburg Chronicle*, November 26, 1910. The inn was also the scene of a boxing match c. 1906. From the collections of Joseph Prah and Betty Hagey Herald.••

The towns of Spring Garden and Alvira in Gregg Township were eliminated when 9,000 acres were appropriated for the Letterkenny Ordnance (now the Allenwood Federal Prison) in World War II. All that remains are memories and views like these: the dam at Spring Garden Mill by Thomas Photo, postmarked 1914, and George Sypher's store in Spring Garden, photographed by John D. Swanger c. 1907-1911. Advertising signs include ones for Dr. James Headache Powder, Uneeda Biscuits, A P Buckles Roasted Coffees, and Breinig's Pure Linseed Oil Paints. From the collection of Gary W. and Donna M. Slear.••

The cider mills of Winfield were photographed by one of the town's three shopkeepers, Malinda Drumm. The postmark is 1916. Mrs. Drumm's store was featured in another of her cards postmarked in 1913 or 1915. From the collection of Gary W. and Donna M. Slear.•

Mill Dam,
Spring Garden Pa.
Thomas, Photo.

George A. Sypher's Store, Spring Garden, Pa.

CIDER MILLS WINFIELD PA.

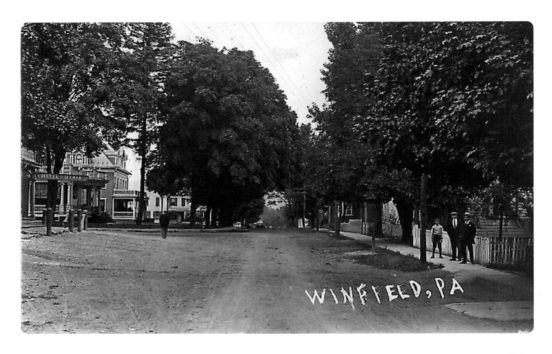

ABOVE Sarah Haines sent this spring/summer view of Winfield's Main Street (including the Hotel Hyman and the Levi Rooke mansion, both on the left) as a New Year's greeting to her brother, who was living in Sunbury. She wrote, "I received your card. to [sic] bad I didn't get down to see you. I had intended to come down on Saturday but now I have a bad cold and the pavements are icy. I would be afraid to start out. we had a nice Christmas we took dinner with the Mahlens. I hope you are well. I wish you all a happy New Year. All come to see me." The view was another taken by Malinda Drumm. From the collection of Gary W. and Donna M. Slear.

The "New Cameron House" (formerly the Revere House, built in 1832, and most recently the Hotel Lewisburger) stood at the northeast corner of Market and Second Streets, Lewisburg. The postmark is 1913. From the collection of Thomas R. Deans.•

The Company A, 12th Regiment National Guard Armory at 221-237 South Third Street, Lewisburg, was the scene of various social events as noted in the local newspapers: "The Ladies Aid Society of the United Evangelical Church served a fine dinner at a moderate price in the Armory on New Year's day," observed the *Mifflinburg Telegraph*, January 4, 1907; "Miss Mabel Laubenstein will hold a Masquerade Dance, in the Armory Hall for her select dancing class on Saturday evening, April 16. Only those receiving tickets will be admitted. A prize will be given to the best dressed couple, also to the one having the most comical costume," remarked the *Lewisburg Chronicle*, April 10, 1910; and "The Lewisburg Chair Works will give their second annual ball in the Armory next Friday morning. Dr. C. S. Jacquemin's full orchestra, just recently organized will furnish music for the occasion," noted the *Lewisburg Chronicle*, November 26, 1910. The Armory was built in 1886 and razed in 1925. This card had a stamped monogram, "S G," in the lower left corner. From the collection of the Union County Historical Society #87.7.10.•

A pretzel is prominently placed in the window of Sholtz and Kaiser Bakery and Confectionery on Market Street, Lewisburg, while a large optical sign hangs in the adjacent clock and watch store. Fresh oysters are promoted as well, both on the street light/sign and on an attached building sign. Merchants and customers assembled for the photograph taken by Edwin S. Heiser some time after 1907. His embossed stamp, "DR. E. S. HEISER/LEWISBURG, PA," is on the card as well. From the collection of the Union County Historical Society #90.13.4.•

Several snow scenes were photographed by Edwin S. Heiser in 1911. The cards show Heiser's neighbor, young Fegley Hopp, in front of 325 Market Street, Lewisburg. This photograph looks east, and has Heiser's druggist standard at the edge of the shoveled sidewalk. From the collection of Helen Hopp.•

ABOVE J. and Hazel M. Burrey's residence and store in Vicksburg were photographed by Stephen B. Horton. The Burrey store sold groceries, coal, lumber, roofing, shoes, drugs, and fertilizer until it closed in 1958. Anderson's Big Store in Buffalo Cross Roads was also photographed by Horton, whose various Buffalo Cross Roads views were the only cards of his offered in both real photo and black-and-white photolithographic versions. From the collections of Joseph Prah and Gary W. and Donna M. Slear.

TOP RIGHT The Commercial Hotel (also known as Young's Hotel) in Mifflinburg was renamed the Buffalo Valley Inn in 1913, a year before it was photographed by Grover Bierly for this postcard. A temperance inn, the new owners hoped to have it patronized by ". . . our home people and by 'strangers and travelers' — commercial men who like good 'feed' and cozy, sleep-inviting beds," according to the *Mifflinburg Telegraph*, March 9, 1913. The January 30, 1920, *Telegraph* noted since the inn had been sold again and renamed the New Buffalo Valley Inn, ". . . upon the maturing of Mr. Hassenplug's plans, Mifflinburg will have one of the finest and most up-to-date Hotels in Central Pennsylvania." Just west of the Buffalo Valley Inn, which was at Chestnut and Fifth Streets, were Hooker's Restaurant and a barber shop. From the collection of Gary W. and Donna M. Slear.

Margaret Reish Haire stands beside the popcorn machine in front of J. F. Dale's Confectionery and the Independent Order of Odd Fellows at 368/370 Chestnut Street, Mifflinburg, c. 1906-1908. From the collection of Katherine Roush. •

A Grover Bierly postcard of the Mifflinburg High School, c. 1914, is marked "Sample #33" on the card's back. Snow scenes are not common, yet another snow scene exists of the school that includes some of the teachers in the foreground. From the collection of the Union County Historical Society #85.7.5. •

BUFFALO VALLEY INN MIFFLINBURG PA.

J.F DALES CONFECTIONARY

O.O.F.

WINTER MIFFLINBURG HIGH School #33

Ruhl & Watson's box factory in Millmont burned down on December 27, 1912. It had employed between twenty and thirty men, one of whom was the photographer, Urs H. Eisenhauer. This card is dated between 1907 and 1912. From the collection of Delphia Shirk.•

The Glen Iron Hotel (#77) was one of Stephen B. Horton's earliest postcards and is dated 1907. The hotel, which was built by Frank Church c. 1900, was operated by his wife, Anna, after his death. Sam Dunlap, who is seen on the card, was the bartender. On the right are Anna and her niece, Alice. As reported in the *Mifflinburg Telegraph*, July 11, 1913, this was the site of attempted arson. An arsonist successfully destroyed the Glen Iron Furnace that year. From the collection of Gary W. and Donna M. Slear.

RIGHT H. R. Mitchell's store in Millmont•, Shirks' store in Hartleton, and W. S. Burd's store in Swengel were taken by Stephen B. Horton c. 1907-1911. The general store in Forest Hill, which Ammon Lutz opened in 1847, was photographed sixty years later, also by Horton.• From the collections of Delphia Shirk, Gary W. and Donna M. Slear, and Ronald P. and Beatrice S. Dreese.

J.F. Mitchell Store, Millmont, Pa. #72 Horton, Photo

W.S. Burd & Co. Swengel Pa. Horton Photo #93

#112, L.H. Miller's Store, Forest Hill, Pa., Horton Photo

#31   The Willows, Buffalo Creek
Near Mifflinburg, Pa.

Around the Bend/Leisure Time

Sense of place in postcard views was not confined to edifices but embraced the wide variety of local landscape: from the drama of Blue Hill's profile on the Susquehanna to the intimacy of the bend and dip of a rural road. Some locations like McClure's "Meadow" along Bull Run on University Avenue in Lewisburg, "The Willows" in Mifflinburg, or Arbutus Lane south of Lewisburg on River Road were photographed many times. They were rendered in many different versions: real photos, cyanotypes, black-and-white or color photolithographs, which were sometimes romanticized with the addition of a night sky and full moon. The numerous versions of such places indicate their significance for many people.

Many of the more intimate or small-scale views of the landscape also give an insight into leisure activities during the century's first decades, as did the newspapers' "Personal" columns. Seasonally, there were Mifflinburg's community picnic and sing, corn and marshmallow roasts at Hairy John's in the Seven Mile Narrows, husking bees, Hallowe'en revelry,[39] belsnickling, sleighing, and skating — which was especially good when the Susquehanna River froze over for fifty-nine consecutive days in 1918, followed by a seventy-four-day stretch in 1919.

Taffy pulls, huckleberry picking, chestnuting, chicken and waffle suppers, chicken and corn dinners,[40] a spelling bee at the Rand School complete with "eats," as well as fishing, frog hunting and gigging were activities focused on food gathering or food consumption. "The boys are now scamping after maple sugar sap. Good luck to them, accompanied by the hope that they may not trip on a trespass notice," noted the *Mifflinburg Telegraph*, March 10, 1911.

The musically inclined could join an orchestra or band. If not, local people could hear others perform at Sankey Hall in Mifflinburg, or in Lewisburg at Bucknell or the Opera House (formerly the Music Hall). In these halls residents could see a musical comedy with Eva Tanguay, watch "When Knighthood was in Flower" or Carrie Nation wielding her temperance hatchet, or participate in a Republican rally. The town's assembly balls were held at the Armory until the mid-1920s. "The tone for this polite form of entertainment was discreetly underplayed and very proper," commented historian Charles Snyder, "...for it took place in the day of quiet elegance, formal calls, calling cards, dance programs, and social protocol, a day doomed to banishment after Word War I."[41]

There were also family reunions at Brook Park, Brouse's Grove, and the Hironimus Church, with games of croquet or quoits. There were men's activities such as fishing at Cat Bird Island, train rides in mixed company to Tea Springs, or buggy or automobile rides in the countryside with the family. For the more athletic there were baseball and later football, swimming, hiking, bicycling, and ballooning, as well as square dances at the Lyric in Mifflinburg. For men there were the Independent Order of Odd Fellows, the Sons of the American Revolution, the Free and Accepted Masons of Pennsylvania, the Knights of the Golden Eagle, the Modern Woodmen, the Red Men, the Patriotic Order of the Sons of America, and the Loyal Order of the Moose. Most fraternal groups were active until after World War I, when the veterans' groups became more popular. For women there were the Civic Club, the DAR, the Shakespeare Club, the Atheneum, and the Twentieth Century Club. For young people there were the Campfire Girls in addition to the Boy Scouts and Girl Scouts.

Wildwood and Wolfland were names of favorite destinations then and now. Sugar Camp too was popular, as noted in the *Mifflinburg Telegraph*, August 11, 1905: "Old sugar camp by Penns Creek is now alive with the usual annual gathering of campers from town, vicinity and their friends from a distance. We wish them a merry health promoting time." Many of the postcards from 1905 to 1935 showed rural America at play.

Favorite scenic spots in Lewisburg and Mifflinburg were the banks of Buffalo Creek where black willows grew. Real photo postcards of these settings were converted into black-and-white as well as colored photolithographic versions — sometimes with moonlight effects added. This Grover Bierly card (#31) from 1914 shows the willows standing erect. Most versions show the willows noticeably bent. From the collection of Ronald Nornhold.•

Two young men and a harnessed dog sit on an Indian motorcycle in "Weiker" some time after 1907. This is the only Union County card found to date that has a motorbike pictured. The postcard was found in Edwin S. Heiser's postcard collection and may have been taken by him. Another card taken at Weikert has his name stamped on the back side. From the collection of Joan Sample.

An excursion like this on the White Deer & Loganton narrow gauge railroad would have been similar to another mentioned in the *Mifflinburg Telegraph*, September 8, 1911: "The White Deer and West Milton Sunday school picnic to be held Sept. 2 at Tea Springs, has been postponed until Sept. 9th on account of the wet weather." Tea Springs excursions remained popular while the line operated between 1906 and 1916. The White Deer & Loganton Railroad connected Buffalo Valley to Sugar Valley. The line was never profitable. From the collection of Gary W. and Donna M. Slear.

The Mosey Inn, located possibly along Buffalo Creek, was photographed by Mary Barber Hagey in the 1920s. One of the postcards shows Mary's sister, Alice, holding a camera, along with Mary's children, William and Dorothy, (extreme left and right). From the collection of Betty Hagey Herald.••

TOP RIGHT This card by Will Bartol was taken on Penns Creek west of Pardee, Hartley Township, at a spot called Camp Thomas. Bucknell seniors often partied there at the end of their final term. From the collection of Gary W. and Donna M. Slear.

"Sunny Side," a rustic cottage along the Susquehanna River at Winfield, was photographed by Winfield shopkeeper Malinda Drumm some time after 1906. From the collection of Joan Sample.•

BOTTOM RIGHT R. Frank Feese's "Katoochqua Cottage" was situated along the west branch of Buffalo Creek on Mifflinburg's west side (near the Industrial Park). Katoochqua was near the swimming hole called "Horsey," one of three ("Sheepy" and "Poopy Deckers" were the others) where young boys gathered to swim in the early 1900s. Other camps were nearby; many sustained damage through repeated flooding. This postcard was sent as an invitation on July 16, 1910, to Mrs. Lee Francis Lybarger and her sisters, reminding them to come there on July 21 at 7:30. Photographer John C. Slear made and marketed a black-and-white photolithographed card of Katoochqua that includes Mr. Feese and friends. From the collection of Gary W. and Donnna M. Slear.

"SUNNY SIDE" WINFIELD, PA.

Penns Creek, looking east.
New Berlin, Pa.

VIEW NEAR LAURELTON

Road back
of Observatory

"Penns Creek, looking east. New Berlin, Pa." was written on this New Berlin card prior to 1907. The card is rare because it looks east rather than west toward Jack's Mountain. A view looking west was a real photo postcard made prior to 1907 and then produced in a black-and-white photolithographic version for New Berlin merchant Frank H. Maurer. From the collection of Ronald Nornhold. •

If it were not marked "A VIEW NEAR LAURELTON, PA.," this Penns Creek scene, postmarked 1912, would be fairly hard to place. From the collection of the Union County Historical Society #90.21.11. •

Thomas Photo of Shamokin developed this "Crossing the Mountain, Allenwood, Pa." c. 1910. From the collection of Thomas R. Deans.•

Rapid Run near Forest Hill was likely a pleasant place for a walk c. 1907 or later. From the collection of Ronald Nornhold.•

BOTTOM LEFT "The Road back of Observatory" was Seventh Street as it left the Bucknell University campus and headed toward the Susquehanna River. The Strohecker farm on River Road as well as Montour Ridge are visible. The card was produced by Edwin S. Heiser before 1907 and is part of his series of scenic views of the Susquehanna. The river was a popular spot as noted by the *Lewisburg Chronicle*, August 28, 1909, "The hot days of the past week caused a swarm of swimmers to seek the cooling waters of the river. At every bathing pier a throng of splashing, diving, laughing bathers could be seen. Coach Huskins was busy with half a dozen pupils. Youngsters for miles about were puddling in the shallows. Young men and women dunked each other. Doctors, lawyers and teachers tried boyhood tricks again. In the evenings scores of working men refreshed themselves after the labors of the day. Altogether the fascination of the Susquehanna seemed to equal those of the old ocean." From the collection of the Union County Historical Society #92.9.91.135.

Camp Skidoo Cat Bird Island.

DEAD GAMERS ALLENWOOD PA.

Stone Villa Haven, Route 15, R. D. 3, Lewisburg, Pa.

ABOVE College Park Motel, Sunset Village, and Stone Villa Haven (CVC Construction) were new spots to spend one's leisure time in the 1930s and later — as a traveler to or going through the area. This is one of two real photo postcards taken at Stone Villa Haven, which was built c. 1930. Its mountain-stone cabins were located three and one-half miles north of Lewisburg, on what was then called Route 404 (Route 15). The cabins had electric lights, private showers and toilets, outside cooking facilities, and picnic tables. Stone Villa Haven was open all year. A series of black-and-white photolithographic cards was also issued by the proprietors, John and Libby Hamler. From the collection of the Union County Historical Society #91.40.11.

LEFT Male enclaves included Camp Skidoo on Cat Bird Island (near Winfield), complete with tents, eating tables, and a chef wearing a toque. Men could go there for the day and pay by the meal. Five different views of Camp Skidoo were taken by Stephen B. Horton, while three views of the Dead Gamers in Allenwood were taken by the Wilson Studio from Milton. The correspondent on the Dead Gamers card noted, "Baloon [sic] did not get far. hit tree and Burned up. Allenwood 1909." • From the collection of Ronald Nornhold.

LEFT Edwin S. Heiser photographed the plane of stunt flyer Sargent Edward Shaffer while it was stuck in a muddy field in Lewisburg on May 22, 1919. Five hundred people waited two hours in Mifflinburg for Shaffer to arrive and perform as planned. As reported in the *Mifflinburg Telegraph* on May 30, "He [Shaffer] waited over an hour for the field to dry out and then attempted a 'take off' in order to come to Mifflinburg. The machine however, refused to leave the ground and crashed into a fence while going at the rate of 70 miles an hour." From the collection of Joan Sample. •

A postcard sent from Winfield on August 1, 1909 is addressed to Miss Gertrude Burns of Winfield. The correspondent, Frank, wrote, "Come down to see the camp this evening and bring three lady friends along." Camp Moxie, presumably in the Winfield area, was photographed complete with Moxie advertisements as well as lanterns blowing in the breeze. From the collection of Ronald Nornhold.•

Several postcard views were made of costumed Hallowe'en revelers in White Deer by Mary Barber Hagey in the 1920s. From the collection of Betty Hagey Herald.••

I Was There When It Happened

Accidents along the train tracks, burglaries, suicides, mishaps involving buggies or automobiles or even airplanes, as well as fires were fodder for the local newspapers when they were not discussing politics or promoting the newest business. Headlines included "Young Man Attacked by a Vicious Bull" [in Allenwood],[42] "A NARROW ESCAPE FROM DEATH BY LION" [when the Johnny Jones Circus came to the area],[43] "BIG BLAZE AT MAZEPPA/Seven Homes, Store Room, Four Barns, Black Smith Shop, Meat Market, etc, Destroyed," and "The Morning After . . ."[44] Later photographs illustrated the devastation wrought when both the Mazeppa Reformed and Lutheran and the Mazeppa Evangelical Churches were devastated by a "hurricane."[45]

Although some disasters were natural, others were the result of carelessness, such as the time Luther Pentycoffe of Black Run burned brush on a windy day and set off a series of fires. Fires were in fact so numerous in 1912 that suspicions of arson were voiced. An earlier fire at one of the area's main employers, the Lewisburg Chair Factory (Pennsylvania House), on July 31, 1905, saw the two-story packing house destroyed and with it over 25,000 finished chairs. The firm's production was set back a month or more. The *Lewisburg Chronicle* suggested that the town extend fire plugs to be within easy reach of the plant and thereby make a quicker response possible. In an editorial in its September 16, 1905, issue, the paper said:

The Lewisburg town council did a commendable thing at the last regular meeting when it decided to afford fire protection to the Lewisburg Chair Works …Owing to the lack of fire protection and in view of the recent disastrous fire at their plant, the Chair Company was considering a proposition from a well-known 'manufacturing' city in the lower part of the state. The Company will stay here if adequate fire protection is given the plant. Through the enterprise of a progressive town council, backed by a petition from heavy taxpayers …the town council met the issue …and now the plant will likely stay in Lewisburg, the *Chronicle* is glad to have had its share in the movement.

Before the construction of the Northeastern Federal Penitentiary, the Lewisburg Chair Factory was the largest business in the county seat, employing 500 people when operating at full capacity.

Incendiary events were often photographed and produced as cards. More rare were cards of a train

On November 6, 1911, there was a train wreck on the Lewisburg & Tyrone Railroad near Lindale. A photograph was taken at the site. Mrs. Libby, the correspondent, wrote to her son in Michigan, "Here is a picture of the wreck Warren E. & Ammon S. are on. The rest are some passengers and the train crew." Lindale was a flag stop in western Union County as were Cherry Run, Thomas Dam, Libby, and Trail's End. Another train wreck that was the subject of a real photo postcard occurred at Cherry Run, where a male passenger drowned in Penns Creek. From the collection of Delphia Shirk.•

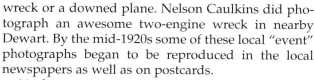

wreck or a downed plane. Nelson Caulkins did photograph an awesome two-engine wreck in nearby Dewart. By the mid-1920s some of these local "event" photographs began to be reproduced in the local newspapers as well as on postcards.

Airplanes were mentioned in the *Chronicle* and *Telegraph* as early as 1915, in large part because of the Lewisburg aviator and inventor, John Cromley, who

was testing his new monoplane that summer. More frequently, eyes began to turn skyward to see the mail planes that were heard as they crossed over Buffalo Valley on their way to New York or Chicago. An emergency landing field was built at Hartleton, and starting in 1925 night beacons were erected east of it near New Berlin and west of it near the Laurelton State Village.[46] Night air mail service was about to begin. As anticipated, these air flights were not without incident, and one crash near Weikert was the subject of a real photo postcard.

The Lewisburg Chair Factory (Pennsylvania House) as it looked during the fire of October 30, 1911. From the collection of the Union County Historical Society #92.9.92.68. •

ABOVE AND TOP RIGHT The burning of the center portion of Old Main at Bucknell University on August 27, 1932, was photographed at several stages and made into postcards. Destroyed in the 4:40 a.m. blaze were the geological and biological collections of Dr. Nelson Davis as well as many musical instruments. Fire fighters came to Lewisburg to fight the blaze from Sunbury, Northumberland, Milton, Watsontown, and Mifflinburg. It was the last fire in which Lewisburg's Silsby Steamer was used, pumping water to Old Main from a fireplug located on the 300 block of Market Street. From the collection of Gary W. and Donna M. Slear. • •

RIGHT These are two of three views of the fire at the Hartman Building, located at 370 Chestnut Street, Mifflinburg. The fire began at 10:50 a.m. on December 26, 1912, starting in the building's rear (or alley) end; it gutted or severely damaged the furniture and casket business of Mr. L. W. Strunk, the Crescent Lodge No. 179 of the Odd Fellows, as well as the Hartline and Shively candy/bakery store. Neighboring buildings had smoke or water damage. From January 25 until March 8, 1913, the three-story brick building was reclaimed, and the various businesses were operating again in April. From the collection of Billy and Lindy Mattern.

ABOVE The New Berlin Hotel was photographed both before and after a devastating fire there on December 8, 1912. The building had been constructed for Christopher Seebold c. 1798. It was run as the Union Hotel by Michael Kleckner until 1904. When the blaze began at 11:45 p.m., only the proprietor, Edward Rehrer, and two others were at the hotel. Before outside help could arrive, the fire spread from the basement and was out of control. Fortunately, it had rained earlier that night and there was no wind; otherwise, the fire might have consumed other buildings in New Berlin. A year and a half later, there was a suspicious fire at New Berlin's Central Hotel, and its owner, A. M. Herman, was charged with arson. From the collection of Gary W. and Donna M. Slear.

RIGHT The Lewisburg Opera House (formerly the Music Hall) was photographed after the fire of December 27, 1908. The building was constructed in 1869 by Henry O. Swartz of Philadelphia and remodeled in 1904 by its second owner, Henry Eyer Spyker, with a seating capacity of 1,000. The Opera House was the largest center for entertainment in the area. The blaze was contained primarily to this building, which included the dental office of Dr. W. R. Roland, C. Oberdorf's plumbing business, the Opera House Cafe, and the local Masonic Lodge; only part of one adjacent house was burned. The Opera House was destroyed, and the loss was estimated at $50,000; but as its insurance coverage was only $15,000, it was never rebuilt. A very small section of its brick wall remains at the east end of the present municipal parking lot. From the collection of the Union County Historical Society #92.9.91.107 and 87.7.2.

As early as 1907, teamster Clifford Eyer posed with the William Cameron Engine Company's Silsby Steam Pumper (purchased in 1874), which was used the night of the Opera House fire. The station house (1877) was on South Fourth Street, behind the Opera House. A new fire station was built on North Fifth Street in 1966, and the old one was leveled to make way for a municipal parking lot in 1969. From the collection of the Union County Historical Society #92.9.91.136. •

Lewisburg Fire Jan. 1909

Take My Picture, Please

Individuals were often photographed by family, friends, or a semi-professional like Urs H. Eisenhauer. People rarely posed inside. They were more likely photographed on their front porch, by the yard gate, with a favorite pet or horse, or out in the field. Their diverse occupations were illustrated as well when they posed at work — as quarrymen, sawyers, railroad workers, schoolmistresses, farmers, firemen, construction workers, drovers, millers, distillers, barbers, and postal carriers. The camera, like the tape recorder of the 1960s and the video camcorder of the 1980s, had become commonplace in the 1910s, and people were accustomed to being "snapped" in this manner.

ABOVE "Present for Mrs. George Catherman" is written on the back of the card by Urs H. Eisenhauer c. 1909-1911. From the collection of Tony Shively.

J. T. Church's workers posed on top of the Glen Iron Furnace (formerly the Berlin Iron Works) in July 1909. Glen Iron was the site of ironworks as early as the 1820s. The furnace suffered a series of fires in 1887, 1892, and 1903, followed by one that was set by arsonists on July 6, 1913. John T. Church was involved in numerous openings and closings of the furnace, including the time it was put back in operation in 1905, close to the time this photo was taken. The furnace closed for the final time in the 1920s. A single card by Stephen B. Horton, postmarked 1913, shows additional furnace buildings. From the collection of Gary W. and Donna M. Slear.

The Kostenbader family posed for a portrait at their spring house on their farm in Kelly Township as early as 1907. On the reverse is written "1 doz" — perhaps for an order. Another view showed the family at their saw mill. From the collection of Gary W. and Donna M. Slear. •

Joel Reish, who is poised with an account book and pencil, and Cling Reish (second from right) are seated with others at the Reish Distillery on Rapid Run near Forest Hill. Joel was the grandson of the distillery's founder, Daniel Reish, who had come to Union County from Berks County. Joel's father, Benival, also operated Forest House at the foot of the Fourteen Mile Narrows. Joel and his brother, James, ran the distillery until 1920. This group portrait, taken as early as 1907, includes small items such as a pocket watch (hanging on a tree), a purse, and a dollar bill. From the collection of Billy and Lindy Mattern. •

Glen Iron Furnace. R.B.t. Jul 4, 1901.
By J.T. Church.

Men posed at the Lewisburg Condensed Milk Company (Bechtel's Dairy Creamery Building) on Buffalo Road, Lewisburg. The photograph was taken some time between 1907 and 1921, when the company employed as many as 150 people making butter, cheese, and condensed milk. From the collection of Kenneth A. and Dorothy G. Reish.•

A wagon filled with bark for tanning in Millmont was photographed at the time a report appeared in the *Lewisburg Chronicle*, June 9, 1906: "Pennsylvania furnished more bark for tanning than any other state in the nation. Of the 766,268 cords of hemlock bark used by the tanneries in 1905, Pennsylvania furnished 379,773 cords; of 293,758 of oak used, Pennsylvania provided 49,903 or a total of 426,676 in a grand total of 1,060,026 in all the states." From the collection of the Union County Historical Society #85.15.5.

TOP RIGHT Men were photographed at work with their stone crusher in a small quarry near Millmont in 1907, while others were photographed at an Allenwood quarry as early as 1907. From the collections of Delphia Shirk and Gary W. and Donna M. Slear.••

BOTTOM RIGHT Charles Musser, Isaac Moyer, and others were photographed working on the race for Rocky's Mill off Buffalo Creek east of Mifflinburg. A grain mill, established there in 1789, burned down in 1971. At the time of this photograph, Rocky's Mill was run by the Voneida and Miller families.The covered bridge in the background has its side painted with an advertisement for "Freedman Clothier and Shoe Dealer." The date 1912 is inscribed in the recently-cast concrete center buttress. From the collection of Gary W. and Donna M. Slear.•

"Stone Crusher"   Millmont, Pa.,

U. H. EISENHAUER PHOTO MILLMONT PA.

Postscript

Until the end of this project, people were still bringing to our attention photographs taken and developed on postcard stock by their family members. These family collections, often large, were usually postcards which had neither messages nor postmarks as they were never sent through the post office; they were not identified on their face by title. Rather, the cards were identifiable by connections to familiar places and people. If taken out of context or left unidentified, these cards would, in most instances, lose most of their meaning. With the exception of the Hallowe'en revelers, the boxing match, the train station interior (all illustrated here), these family cards would be relegated to the "general real photo cards" at any postcard or ephemera show to which card collectors go in search of additional "local" cards. The postcards would be stripped of their rich cultural context.

The Hagey/Herald and the Heiser/Sample collections are just that — wonderful and late-surfacing family collections. The former, primarily the work of Mary Barber Hagey, was photographed in White Deer, Union County, or at other local places with a family connection. The latter, primarily the work of Lewisburg druggist and photographer Edwin S. Heiser, included some of his "commercial" cards but mostly consisted of more personal subject matter:

three interior shots of his store, views of Market Street taken from in front of his store during snow storms, and street paving work. His own postcard album had cards of Central Oak Heights and the United Evangelical Home — evidence of his ties to area Methodism. His album also had selected real photo postcards by photographers Malinda Drumm and John D. Swanger, among others.

While card collectors will still make the occasional single find, it will be the discovery of such family collections in the future that will add substantially to our knowledge and appreciation of rural America in the first decades of the twentieth century.

[1] Samuel Elliott Morrison, *The Oxford History of the American People* (New York: Oxford University Press, 1965), 773, 811-12, 888-93, called the last three decades of the nineteenth century "The Gilded Era" as "… it was a robust. fearless, generous era, full of gusto and joy of living, affording wide scope to individual energy and material creation." In Union County, Pennsylvania, the Gilded Era was evidenced by the restrained elegance of formal balls, teas, and receptions, which were the practice of the old-time Lewisburg families. At Eli Slifer's home, Delta Place, outside Lewisburg, there were a stable of Kentucky thoroughbred horses, flocks of guinea hens, as well as peacocks preening on the lawn. Morrison called the next period, 1902 to 1939, "The Great Change," wrought in large part by the introduction and wide acceptance of the automobile; and he labeled the beginning of the century "The Progressive Era."

ABOVE Phoebe Vorse was photographed in her garden at the corner of North Second and St. Mary Streets, Lewisburg. From the collection of Gary W. and Donna M. Slear. •

Charly Kerwell of Laurelton, with his sheep, geese, and gun, was photographed by Urs H. Eisenhauer c. 1909-1911. From the collection of the Union County Historical Society #79.469.2.

Lewisburg children posed with a pet cat on a card sent July 17, 1909. From the collection of Kenneth A. and Dorothy G. Reish. •

Pauline Shirk posed with her dog on her porch in Hartleton c. 1907-1911. From the collection of Delphia Shirk. •

Several different portraits were taken of Charlie and his horse, Maude, near Lochiel on the Old Turnpike c. 1907-1908. The view looks east at the Duck (Kissinger) family farm. From the collection of Kenneth A. and Dorothy G. Reish.

[2] Card from the Gary W. and Donna M. Slear collection, Lewisburg, Pa.

[3] Card from the Ronald Nornhold collection, Troxelville, Pa.

[4] See Fred W. Lindig's advertisement circular, p. 13, John Van Buskirk collection, Lewisburg, Pa.

[5] Over 800 bicycles were registered to Union County residents in 1899 (population 17,592 in 1900). Charles Snyder, *Union County Pennsylvania: A Bicentennial History* (Lewisburg, Pa.: Union County Bicentennial Commission, 1976), 132.

[6] See also Reverend A. Stapleton's address at the dedication of the Maclay monument as it appeared in its entirety, *Lewisburg (Pa.) Chronicle*, October 24, 1908, pp. 1, 4; Snyder, *Union County*, 53-54, for more on Samuel Maclay and his brother, William Maclay.

[7] See *Mifflinburg (Pa.)Telegraph*, August 1, 1919, p. 1, for coverage of the dedication ceremony.

[8] *Mifflinburg Telegraph*, April 12, 1924.

[9] *Mifflinburg Telegraph*, January 5, 1906, p. 1, described in great detail the order and participants in the Mifflinburg event: "Chief Marshal Martin C. Reed and Aids Stitzer and Getgen, Lewisburg Cornet Band, Horsemen in fantastic garb to the number of 20 or more — a scene exciting the admiration and hearty laughter of all, Aid D. B. Moss, Veteran Soldier Samuel G. Grove as 'Uncle Sam,' in wagon driven by a colored driver, his son Fred. A fine and appropriate representation, Schnure Post of Grand Army Boys on foot with their handsome new flag at the front, and each member carrying small flags, Foster Post of Mifflinburg in conveyances with their pretty flag in front, Mayor Wm. A Doebler and his Aid, Milton M. Schoch, Hon. Jas. R. Ritter and three or more friends in carriage, Wagon with men in fantastic costumes, Aid F. B. Brubaker, Hobo Band with seven-foot gentleman as Drum Major (Charlie Laudenslager) all in fantastic garb, Stitzer & Reed Drum Corps, Young men from Lewisburg, their faces well covered with burned cork, carrying a banner inscribed "West End Livery" (Irwin's), Harry Gensburg's Wagon, descriptive of cheap and good clothing, Three persons in fantastic costumes with placards on their backs telling the good quality of W. F. Brown's vehicles [buggies], Beckley's Milk Wagon with placards advertising Brown's Wagons being good for 22,000 miles, and also the superior milk sold by T. H. Beckley. "Baby Walter" occupied a prominent seat on this wagon, Henry J. Cromley's Wagon containing musical instruments, sewing machines, etc., Cowan Cornet Band, Chas. E. Kerstetter, livery man in the wagon, his horse blanketed, on which was inscribed something appropriate for G. W. Young's implement store; this followed by Mr. Young's wagon containing implements, Mr. Hartman's wagon containing fine furniture — a pretty kitchen cabinet, etc., Jas. Hoover's display — man and woman in fantastic regalia, Heiter's Barber Shop Wagon — men engaged in shaving and hair cutting, a very cute affair, Several Fantastics on horseback. Strunk's Store Exhibit on large wagon — a fine display; followed by his Delivery Wagon, Three Fantastic Boys in Wagon drawn by Steans' pony, the latter's legs being well leggined, Wagon representing Merchant Bibighaus' business — neat display of shoes, boots and rubber goods, two wagons with fantastic occupants, Eureka Bakery Wagon — a great hit, Golden Eagle Band, Solomon R. Hoffman in his Rural Free Delivery Wagon No 1, the same being handsomely festooned with 'Old Glory,' Aid Horace G. Ewing, The Wagon of Mr. C. T. Valentine, the Harness Maker, Fantastics in Wagon, John Klinger in Wagon telling of his cigars and tobacco, Aid Jno. E. Bibighaus, Mr. L. W. Strunk's Wagon, with fine display of furniture, Merrill Well___n Wagon advertising goods and the Grand Union Tea Co., A Wagon containing Kegs, whether to represent the quality of the kegs or that which they contained or did not at the moment contain, we cannot say.

Better inquire of the 'owner' of the float for correct information, Boys with horns, in wagon, all fantastically dressed, Aid G. L. Reish, Wagon from country with wood choppers and sawyers. Wagon with Fantastics, Star Buggy Works Wagon, Wagon with Fantastics, all having pig faces, Wagon from Country, W. L. Hoffman's Wagon, containing roofed house, plumber's supplies, tinware, etc., The Mifflinburg Creamery Wagon, Gast's fine store display on large wagon, Hopp Carriage Co. Display Wagon, containing blacksmith shop with men at work, Foster's Feed and Coal Wagon, with coal, Mr. J. H. Garrett's Tea and Spice Wagon, Wagon from Country with grindstone and windmill, Wagon containing a couple just married, Mr. Paul B. Gutelius with wall paper on Ben. Newberry's wagon, E. J. Gutelius' Delivery Wagon, Chas. E. Sechler's Stock Food and Implement Wagon, Fantastics on foot, Brown's Stock Yard Wagon, The twins, with a Bear, creating more fun than one can describe, Two more fantastically attired men on bicycles glided along the line of march creating great sport." The reporter concluded, "Souvenirs of pretzels, fruits, cakes, circulars, etc., etc., were lavishly distributed along the line of march. In the column there were fully 312 persons, quite three-fourths of whom being in masquerade attire."

[10] *Lewisburg Chronicle*, January 8, 1910, p. 1.

[11] "LEWISBURG'S GALA DAY WILL BE NEW YEAR'S DAY/Many Good Prizes Are Offered," *Mifflinburg Telegraph*, December 24, 1915, p. 1.

[12] Ibid.

[13] "The hope and prayer for good weather was fully granted — it could scarcely have been better at this season of the year, which in fact aided in attracting to our prosperous, progressive and growing town, whose gates are ever wide open to those who desire a nice village to live in, and with us aid in its continued prosperity …," proclaimed the *Mifflinburg Telegraph*, January 5, 1906, p. 1. This sentiment was about Mifflinburg, Union County, but could as well is representative of life in many areas of rural America at the turn of the century.

[14] See David Luthy, *The Amish in America: Settlements That Failed, 1840-1960* (Aylmer, Ontario, Canada: Pathway Publishers, 1986), 421-430, for a history of the first Amish settlement which split because of personalities and doctrinal differences.

[15] Other agricultural groups formed within the county from time to time. The *Mifflinburg Telegraph*, January 17, 1913, p. 1, observed that "There will be a meeting of the fruit growers of the county held in the High School room of this place on Saturday afternoon of this week, at 1:30 o'clock. The object of the gathering for the purpose of reorganizing the County Fruit Growers' Society and otherwise stimulating the sentiment in favor of producing better fruit."

[16] *Mifflinburg Telegraph*, September 5, 1919, p. 1.

[17] Pennsylvania's Governor Gifford Pinchot vowed to "get the farmer out of the mud" through his road building program.

[18] See G. Howard Klingman, *Buffalo Valley Telephone Company 1904-1974* (1974); and the reports that appeared in the *Lewisburg Chronicle* between September 17, 1904, and May 14, 1909.

[19] *Mifflinburg Telegraph*, May 14, 1909, p. 1.

[20] *Mifflinburg Telegraph*, January 15, 1925, p. 1.

[21] " 'Cleaning up Around Town'/Lewisburg is putting on its best bib and tucker, for during the next week there be a great host of strangers here to attend the Bucknell Commencement. Lawns are being cut, trimmed and edged. The borough supervisor is cleaning the streets and alleys and everywhere there is an appearance of cleanliness." *Lewisburg Chronicle*, June 18, 1904, p. 1.

[22] *Mifflinburg Telegraph*, August 6, 1915, p. 1.

[23] Eleven-day train excursions to Ocean Grove's Camp Meeting were advertised in the local newspapers that same year, 1909.

[24] Devitt's Camp closed in the 1950s when a tuberculosis treatment center was no longer needed. Devitt transferred its title to St. Peter's Reformed Church, which used the camp as a home for the aged until it was closed in 1968 because it no longer met state standards.

[25] *Mifflinburg Telegraph*, October 12, 1922, p. 1.

[26] The debate about the proposed free bridges was held in newspapers statewide from 1901 until 1905, when the Mohn bill was passed by the state legislature; this allowed the use of state and local funds for the replacement of privately owned and aging structures. Controversy about Lewisburg's free bridge continued well past the bridge's dedication in 1908 and involved a lawsuit pitting the Lewisburg Bridge Company against the Union County and Northumberland County commissioners. The case was finally dismissed in 1910. The *Lewisburg Chronicle*, September 18, 1909, had asked, "Will the taxpayer of Union County call the new bridge that was opened to the public July 1, 1908, a free bridge after being taxed to the tune of 24,060 dollars for our share of the bridge and now file a lawsuit of $200,000 that may cost the county $40,000 more? What constitutes a free bridge?"

[27] "Upon the assumption that mental retardation was hereditary, the institution was conceived as a means of removing female mental defectives of child-bearing age from society, who would otherwise breed and multiply. The school was designed to care for them, and to train them, when feasible, for employment in domestic service and agriculture. Once they were beyond the child-bearing age, the more competent might be paroled, and hopefully, become self-sustaining. The emphasis at the outset, however, seems to have been upon removal and isolation, rather than upon reclamation." Snyder, *Union County*, 246.

[28] *Mifflinburg Telegraph*, February 19, 1931, p. 1.

[29] See Snyder, *Union County*, 32-51, for a detailed description of area transportation links.

[30] The importance of the train was reflected by repeated commentary in the *Mifflinburg Telegraph* from 1905 to 1912: "The people of New Berlin are now very happy, in that trains from Winfield are daily arriving in their town." (June 23, 1905); "New Berlin has finally emerged from her como state and now has railroad connection to the outside world. Everyone come. Bring your friends and enjoy a day in one of the finest and most beautiful towns in the country. You will never regret it." (June 30,1905) [They officially celebrated the New Berlin & Winfield R.R. opening with a twilight concert on July 4]; "On Monday morning of last week the mail was transferred from the star route at Winfield to the New Berlin & Winfield Railroad. New Berlin now gets three mails daily receiving the first and heaviest mail at 9:30 instead of between 2 and 3 p.m." (February 2, 1906); "As the 'Telegraph' predicted some time ago, the enterprising and public spirited citizens of New Berlin have come to the front with their cash, and, as a happy result, their railroad between that point and Winfield is again in running order." (November 8, 1912).

[31] See Charles M. Snyder, *An Era in American Transportation* (Lewisburg, Pa.: The Oral Traditions Project of the Union County Historical Society, 1984).

[32] November 19, 1909.

[33] Susquehanna University in Selinsgrove (est. 1852) and Lycoming College in Williamsport (est. 1812).

[34] See Lewis Edwin Theiss, *Centennial History of Bucknell 1846-1946* (Lewisburg, Pa.: Bucknell University, 1946); J. Orin Oliphant, *The Rise of Bucknell University* (New York: Appleton-Century-Crofts, 1965); I. H. Mauser *History of Lewisburg* (1886; reprint, Lewisburg, Pa.: Union County Historical Society, 1986), which in its chapter on Bucknell contains annotations by the school's former vice-president, John Zeller; Snyder, *Union County*, 106-114.

[35] Now it has 3,710 students, 254 faculty, and 703 staff members with a national reputation of excellence as a university with a liberal arts college and a college of engineering.

[36] Since this was the Great Depression, married female school teachers would have been criticized for bringing in a second income when many families had little or no income.

[37] See Union County Historical Society, comp, *Union County Churches* (Lewisburg, Pa.: Union County Historical Society, 1995).

[38] Interview with Bessie Bates Hoffman, Lewisburg, Pa., April 24, 1976, Oral Traditions Project/Union County Historical Society reel #53, mentioned having chickens and cows in Lewisburg around the turn of the century, "... we really lived like country people [at the corner of North Second and Market Streets]." The Hoffmans butchered pigs in the fall and always had two cows there in the summer.

[39] "Next Monday occurs Halloween, one of the greatest events of the year for jollification, for the young people of our town. Is it a foregone conclusion that as usual Lewisburg will have its many celebrations at different places in town among the student clubs and fraternities and elsewhere. The desire however is that this year all obnoxious actions of a few who seem to find pleasure and fun in committing depredations which result in damage to property or clothing be eliminated," *Lewisburg Chronicle*, October 29, 1910, p. 1.

[40] A sample menu included chicken corn soup, wafers, chicken croquettes, corn oysters, sauce, french fried potatoes, stewed corn, corn on the cob, pickled cabbage, ice cream and cake

[41] Snyder, *Union County*, 98.

[42] *Mifflinburg Telegraph*, September 4, 1914.

[43] *Mifflinburg Telegraph*, September 10, 1915.

[44] *Mifflinburg Telegraph*, September 8, 1916.

[45] *Mifflinburg Telegraph*, July 29, 1926. [The "hurricane" was, most likely, a small localized tornado.]

[46] "The powerful beacon light has already been erected and tests being made nightly, having started on Saturday night, May 2. This accounts for the light that has been seen flashing in the heavens and which has been seen for miles around in this section. This immense light erected on a tower about 125 feet in height, has illuminating qualities of 1,500,000 candle power. Smaller lights will be located at regular distances between each emergency field ...These smaller lights will be 300,000 candle power set on windmill towers fifty-three feet in height and will be operated with current supplied by farm lighting plants. The beacons will revolve about six times a minute, throwing the light about one degree above the horizon, making it unnecessary for the fliers to depend on occasional city or village light or flashes from automobile, street car, or railway traffic... Equipped with magnesium flares, which, supported by small parachutes float in the air for four minutes or more, and with big landing lights on the outer tips of the wings, the mail planes are in good shape to land in the event of motor trouble." *Mifflinburg Telegraph*, May 7, 1925, p. 1.

William "Will" Andrew **Bartol** (1886-1980) received his Bachelor of Science degree from Bucknell University in 1905 and his Master of Science degree two years later. Will grew up in the former Lowry home on University Avenue, Lewisburg. His father, Bucknell professor William C. Bartol, wrote to William Rudisill in Altoona, Pennsylvania, in 1908, "This is one of Will's Camp Thomas pictures." It is likely that other views of Bucknell and Lewisburg were taken by Will Bartol. A card printed by the Roto-graph Co., New York, of "Lovers Retreat, Bucknell University" was also stamped "Wm. A. Bartol, copyright 1909." In 1909 Will Bartol also published a booklet called "Bucknell Traditions," which included a section on the class competitions called "scraps."

E. R. **Bartoo** (c. 1890-1969) was a Bucknell University student who produced eleven or more Lewisburg/Bucknell scenes as postcards; these were stamped "MADE BY E. R. BARTOO/LEWISBURG, PA." on the backs. A resident of Mills, Pennsylvania, Eli Roe Bartoo matriculated with the class of 1911. As a fellow student wrote on a card, "A fellow who is working his way through took these pictures and made up the cards. He came around selling them and I bought a bunch." Perhaps not enough cards were sold, however, as Bartoo did not graduate. Later, Bartoo taught vocational agriculture in several New York schools until he retired in 1954.

As a young man, William "Grover" **Bierly** (c. 1900-d. ?) moved with his mother, Sara, to Mifflinburg in September 1914. Before Grover enlisted in World War I, he produced a wide range of Mifflinburg postcards including streetscapes, "bird's-eye" views, and extensive parade pictures. His shots are usually hand numbered and signed on the card's front, as illustrated on a tree trunk in a 1914 view, "#31 The Willows, Buffalo Creek/Near Mifflinburg, Pa." A single card of Bierly's has been found which used a name stamp on the front of the card. In 1921 Grover Bierly, a tenant of R. E. Newberry's, left Mifflinburg, presumably returning to New York State.

"Blair" was written on the front of a few early Mifflinburg postcards. There were a number of Blairs in the 1910 Mifflinburg census and most were connected with buggy production.

Nelson A. **Caulkins** lived near Mansfield, Tioga County, and photographed many scenes of Pennsylvania's Grand Canyon. As a young man, Caulkins traveled as far away from home as Waterville, New York, as well as to McEwensville, Northumberland County, and Selinsgrove, Snyder County, to take pictures he then produced as postcards. In Lewisburg, Union County, Caulkins took photographs at the 1914 Odd Fellows' parade, as well as at least twenty-seven different views of Lewisburg's World War I homecoming parade in 1919. Caulkins' surname was written on the front of two catastrophic event series, both of which took place in Dewart, Northumberland County: a two-engine train collision on November 23, 1918, and a cyclone in 1919. He was living in Lycoming County as late as 1954.

Nelson Fithian **Davis** (1872-1939) earned both his Bachelor and Master of Science degrees at Bucknell University; he also taught biology there from 1898 to 1939. He lived at 47 South Water Street, Lewisburg. Dr. Davis was an avid photographer who made copies of historical photographs for documentary purposes, used lantern slides for class lectures, and photographed the Bucknell campus and the natural environment. The Nelson Davis Photographic Collection is housed at the Bucknell University Archives. No postcards have Davis' name on them; but at least six of his photographs or glass plates match cyanotype, black-and-white and/or color photolithographic postcards of Shriner's Island (Campbell's Mill), the 1906 Memorial Bridge at Bucknell, the road in back of the Observatory, a Bucknell/State College football game on Loomis Field, as well as a snow scene in front of the Lowry/Bartol house (Psychiatric Services Building).

"Drumm Photo" appears in thin lettering on the front of a card titled "Entrance to Cave/ Stone Quarry Winfield." From at least 1905 through 1910 Malinda S. **Drumm** (1845- d. ?) ran a general store and lived in Winfield. On the back of another postcard was stamped, "Main Street Winfield/Drumm Photo," and the photographer/storekeeper requested William H. Moll, 682 Mahoning Street, Milton, to "Send us 10 loaves more Bread each time till further order. Yours Truly Mrs. M. S. Drumm."

One of the area's most prolific postcard producers was U. H. **Eisenhauer** (1858-1935) who stamped on the front of his cards "U. H. EISENHAUER PHOTO" or "U. H. EISENHAUER PHOTO MILLMONT, PA." Similar block-lettered stamps also were used to identify the

Grover Bierly, second from right, had his photograph taken on his mother's porch in Mifflinburg when he was home on a furlough in 1918. From the collection of Gary W. and Donna M. Slear. •

Sue and Urs H. Eisenhauer had their portrait taken in Millmont, c. 1920, when he was sixty-eight and she was sixty-two years old. The backdrop is similar to that which he often used when taking others' portraits. From the collection of Delphia Shirk.

locations. Postmarks on Eisenhauer cards date from 1909 to 1911. Of Pennsylvania-German parentage, Urs and his wife, Sue, spoke the dialect and lived in their home on the south side of Maple Street in Millmont. Eisenhauer developed his glass negatives in a building behind the house. In 1910, at the time Eisenhauer was especially active with his photography, the county's tax assessor listed him as a carpenter and fifty-two years old; in 1920 Eisenhauer was working at the Ruhl & Watson box factory in Millmont. His postcards are usually homes or hamlets in western Union County. Eisenhauer also photographed New Berlin, which he spelled phonetically "NEW BURLAND" in his stamp; the Twin Churches in Kelly Township; and the construction of the Lewisburg/Mifflinburg Turnpike. He also executed a series of cards in Centerville (Penns Creek) and in Huffer (between Meiserville and Port Trevorton), Snyder County. Two of his views of Hartleton were poorly lithographed by a C. F. Henry, date not known. Eisenhauer also captured the likenesses of many individuals, some of whom posed with their pets or farm animals. He often used backdrops for his group portrait work: fabric stretched by two vertical poles or by ropes, or suspended from a porch ceiling.

A single card from June 1914 of a Flag Day parade in Allenwood is marked "Photo by Fuller." Nothing is known about **Fuller**.

"HALLMAN" appears as an embossed stamp on a single card of the Bergenstock home at Muddy Run, near Mazeppa. The card was made in 1907 or later. Nothing is known about **Hallman**.

Roy W. **Hartman** ran a store in Mifflinburg that sold postcards with his stamp on the back. He is mentioned in the December 8, 1905, *Mifflinburg Telegraph* as "selling pictures."

Dr. Edwin S. **Heiser** (1855-1923) was born in Aaronsburg, Centre County, Pennsylvania, and was a graduate of Jefferson Medical College, Philadelphia. Along with his brother, W. D. Heiser, Edwin purchased the drug store of Sylvanus Bennett at 321 Market Street, Lewisburg, in 1880. He also sold photo supplies and as noted in his obituary, "He loved as well the art of photography, and was one of the best amateur photographers in the State. Nature — the woods and streams, called him to the forest every year…" He traveled abroad and conducted slide shows for local groups.

Heiser had an elaborate embossed stamp, "Dr. E. S. Heiser/Lewisburg, Pa," that often appears on the front of his postcards. A simpler embossed stamp which reads "DR. E. S. HEISER/LEWISBURG, PA." has been found on several cards. Fewer of his cards were stamped in ink on their backs, "DR. E. S. HEISER DRUGS AND PHOTO SUPPLIES/LEWISBURG, PA." Many of Heiser's landscapes were vignetted in an oval format. Advertisements for his business appeared from 1909 to 1921 in *The Blue and Orange* and *The Bucknellian*. Along with his second wife, Ella, and their son, Edwin, Dr. Heiser lived next door to the Fegley Stationery Store (Lewisburg News Agency), which was run by the Fegley/Hopp family. In later years the Hopps produced and sold many Lewisburg postcards in the then-fashionable colored linen (c. 1930-1945) and chrome styles(1945 on).

1907 was earliest postmark on a card of Stephen B. **Horton** (1882- d. ?). He was a boarder from 1908 to 1911 at the West Milton hotel run by George and Clara Fenstermacher. A New Yorker, Horton was a "commercial traveler" or salesman of biscuits. This accounts for his picture-taking in places as widespread as Glen Iron, Laurelton, Forest Hill, Cowan, Mazeppa, Buffalo Cross Roads, Vicksburg, Winfield, Lewisburg, West Milton, New Columbia, and Spring Garden in Union County; also towns like Dalmatia, Mahanoy, Malta, Rebuck, Urban, Paxtonville, Troxelville, and Montandon in Northumberland, Snyder, and Montour Counties. His town views tend not to be streetscapes that looked down a street, but rather streetscapes which featured a particular country store, almost as the building's portrait. Quite likely, storekeepers bought both Horton's biscuits *and* postcards. In 1907 and 1908 Stephen B. Horton was active in the Millmont area prior to the emergence of Urs H. Eisenhauer as a photographer.

Horton's photographic style stands in contrast to that of his chief competitor, U. H. Eisenhauer, who specialized in out-of-door portraiture. Stephen B. Horton rarely took people's portraits, an exception being one of a young man at Yankee Spring, Winfield, Union County, who happened to be the son of the local shopkeeper. Horton usually handwrote the location and "HORTON PHOTO" on the card's front. A few of his cards are stamped in ink on their backs "S. B. HORTON/WEST MILTON, PA." Several of Horton's photographs of Buffalo Cross Roads were issued as photolithographic postcards as well as real photo cards. Horton's name may appear on cards from elsewhere, made after he left this area of Central Pennsylvania.

Arthur R. **Ishiguro** (1887-1956) came to the United States between 1900 and 1915. He was a professional studio photographer who took over John D. Swanger's